NOTHING WASTED

NOTHING WASTED

A MEMOIR

LOSING MY DREAM
TO FIND GOD'S PURPOSE

CATINA VAUGHN

Copyright © 2025 by Catina Vaughn
Nothing Wasted: Losing My Dream to Find God's Purpose

All rights reserved. No part of this book may be reproduced, stored in a retrieval system, or transmitted in any form or by any means—electronic, mechanical, photocopying, recording, or otherwise—without prior written permission of the publisher, except for brief quotations used in reviews or scholarly works.

Published by **Keywords Unlocked Publishers®**
6969 N. Port Washington Road, Suite B150, #1025
Glendale, Wisconsin 53217
keywordsunlockedllc@gmail.com
www.keywordsunlocked.com

Library of Congress Control Number (LCCN): 2025947395
ISBN (Hardcover): 979-8-9990953-1-2
ISBN (Paperback) 979-8-9990953-5-0

Cover design: Keywords Unlocked Publishers®
Interior design & formatting: Keywords Unlocked Publishers®

Printed in the United States of America

Disclaimer: This memoir reflects the author's personal journey and perspectives. While the events are true, some identifying details have been omitted to respect privacy.

Scripture quotations are from The Holy Bible, New International Version® (NIV), New Living Translation® (NLT), King James Version® (KJV), used by permission.

All rights reserved worldwide.

First Edition: November 2025
10 9 8 7 6 5 4 3 2 1

To my beloved Grandmother, Georgia Vaughn, and my cousin, Joyce Vaughn-Burns. I cherish each memory we shared and miss you both dearly.

NOTE TO THE READER

If you have experienced disappointment in life and relationships,

If you have begun your journey with a pure heart and earnest expectations, only to discover that life rarely unfolds as you planned,

If you have felt you were caught in cycles of regret and despondency, convinced you've missed your chance at a happily ever after,

I share my story with you.

If you have needed someone relatable to connect with and draw encouragement from,

If life hasn't gone the way you dreamed—or isn't unfolding the way you're still dreaming—know that God has a way of causing all things to work together for our good.

He reminds us that His dream for us is far greater than anything we could ever imagine.

My prayer is that, as you turn each page, you will find hope, peace with where you are, and renewed faith in your future.

You are my reason.

CONTENTS

NOTE TO THE READER	vii
INTRODUCTION	xiii
CHAPTER 01 Where It All Began	1
CHAPTER 02 The Anointing	9
CHAPTER 03 Favor vs. Fantasy	17
CHAPTER 04 My Dreams Come True	25
CHAPTER 05 A Dream Lost	33
CHAPTER 06 Dreams Attacked	37
CHAPTER 07 A Dream Disturbed	43
CHAPTER 08 A Dream Turned Nightmare	53

CHAPTER 09
The Silent Surrender — 59

CHAPTER 10
What Do You KNOW? — 67

CHAPTER 11
The Departure — 73

CHAPTER 12
The Darkness — 77

CHAPTER 13
The Diagnosis — 83

CHAPTER 14
The Invitation — 87

CHAPTER 15
Miss Fix It — 91

CHAPTER 16
Religion to Relationship — 97

CHAPTER 17
The Reset — 105

CONCLUSION — 113

ACKNOWLEDGMENTS — 115

ABOUT THE AUTHOR — 117

INTRODUCTION

Jeremiah 29:11

When I was a little girl, I dreamed of my "Prince Charming." Like many girls from my generation, I imagined him sweeping me off my feet, making me his wife, and building a life where we would live happily ever after. In my daydreams, my home was always the most beautiful place, surrounded by a crisp white picket fence. *There had to be a white picket fence, right?* That fence wasn't just decoration—it was my picture of safety, love, and protection.

I imagined coming home as an adult, walking up to the house, opening the gate, stepping onto the porch, and standing there admiring the beauty—the sun shining, the flowers blooming, and the trees swaying in the yard. That thought gave me such a warm, satisfying feeling.

Behind the white picket fence was home. My house. My covering. My safe place. My sanctuary. The place where love would abide. A place where I could be free.

A place where I would raise my children, grow old with my

husband, and take care of my family. The place where we would spend holidays, throw birthday parties, and, of course, have barbecues. My home. My life.

By definition, a dream is a cherished aspiration, ambition, or ideal—a strongly desired goal or purpose—and this was mine. But where did I get this dream? Why was I so strongly drawn to marriage and family?

Maybe I was influenced by the culture of the 1980s, where TV sitcoms were more family-centered. I'd watch shows like *Family Matters, Growing Pains, Family Ties*, and, of course, *The Cosby Show*. And then there were the magical influences of Cinderella and The Princess Bride. Maybe even a sprinkle of romance from *General Hospital* and *Days of Our Lives*, which I watched with my grandmother. I mean, who didn't want to be Luke and Laura Spencer, or Bo and Hope Brady?

Holding on to something like that comforted my inner being. This was the vision I had for my life. Whenever I thought of it, I felt warm and fuzzy inside. It made me smile. Have you ever felt that way about something? It's what most people long for. It's what most people strive to feel in their everyday lives.

Everybody tells us to dream, but no one tells us that not all dreams come true—or that some dreams may turn into nightmares. No one tells you that you may have to let one dream die for another to live. And rarely is there any discussion about how other people can *impact your dream*.

There is nothing wrong with having a dream for your life. I think everyone should. However, I want to help someone understand that there may come a time when you have to set aside a dream you have carried in your heart. Maybe you are in that place right now, struggling like I was—nurturing something that was destined to die simply because it was part of your dream. Or maybe you have already walked through it, and you know what it feels like to let go of something you desperately wanted.

It may sound depressing, but as Scripture says, "Better is the end of a thing than the beginning thereof." (Ecclesiastes 7:8, NLT) We must realize that even though we have dreams and ambitions for our lives, God also has something in mind for us. For God's plan to live, our plans may have to die.

We can make our own plans, but the Lord determines our steps. (Proverbs 16:9, NLT)

In this book, I share some of the most precious, heartfelt stories, as well as some of the most challenging times in my life. Writing it has stretched me in ways I never imagined. It has pulled me out of my safe place of silence, broken down the walls I built to protect myself, and made me vulnerable again. For years, rumors circulated—speculations, guesses, and assumptions—and I was not allowed to respond.

God told me, "*Not yet.*" But now, at His instruction, I am inviting you into some of my most private thoughts and experiences. In them, you will see how the hand of God was at work in my life. You'll see how He can turn your mess into a message, use your failures to cultivate greater faith, and show you that "He causes everything to work together for the good of those who love Him and are called according to His purpose." (Romans 8:28, NLT)

Trust me, after the process, you will awaken to something far greater than you could have ever dreamed on your own. Join me on this journey as I share my story—one that begins in the place where my love for God and the church first took root.

CHAPTER 01

Where It All Began

I loved the church. I loved God. And it all started when I was seven years old. My aunt started a church, and the first service was held in my parents' home, in the basement. That moment sparked the beginning of my journey in the ministry of our Lord Jesus Christ. Ever since I can remember, ministry has been an important part of my life. Our lives revolved around it, and the church was always a priority.

In this day and age, it's pretty uncommon to see a church begin in someone's home or basement. Now, there are church launch services with strategic marketing plans, flyers, commercials—the whole nine. But back then, it was just our basement and the saints gathering together. There was something special about it—the people, my pastor, the way she preached, the choir, the charismatic atmosphere. It was amazing, and I was intrigued.

The church atmosphere back then had a familiarity that I couldn't quite articulate, but I know it was the presence of the Lord.

When His presence filled the room, I didn't always understand what was happening, but there was something in me that connected with the Holy Spirit. It was as if we'd known each other before—I knew Him.

Without the accurate dialect or the knowledge of a theologian, I had made a connection with the Creator, the God of the church. This felt like home.

We didn't stay in the basement long. Within a few months, we moved to a storefront church at 1122 W. North Avenue. The church membership began to increase rapidly.

On the walls hung the Church Covenant and the Lord's Prayer. The Church Covenant began like this:

Having been led, as we believe, by the Spirit of God to receive the Lord Jesus Christ as our Savior, and on the profession of our faith, having been baptized in the name of the Father, and of the Son, and of the Holy Ghost, we now in the presence of God, angels, and this assembly, most solemnly and joyfully enter into the covenant with one another as one body in Christ.

We recited this out loud every Sunday, and even though it has been well over 30 years, I can still quote many parts of it verbatim. Every Saturday was dedicated to church preparations. Meetings were held, the choir practiced, and on some Saturdays, the church mothers and some of the women would gather in the kitchen to fry chicken or fish dinners to sell. That's how we raised extra money for the church. This was in the early 1980s—times were different then, and this was what serving in ministry looked like for us. We didn't have a lot of money or people, but we had a heart to serve.

Back then, days were busy and lively! The sizzling sound of the chicken and fish frying, with the occasional popping of grease, filled the air. The smell of Southern-fried cuisine drifted into the sanctuary—along with a bit of smoke. Sounds of chattering and laughter were what you'd hear coming through the door.

My grandmother would be fussing and cracking jokes at the same time. She'd be cooking while others were preparing plates, putting the food into those white Styrofoam to-go boxes. Then the deacons of the church would sit and eat while they waited for the plates to be ready so they could deliver them.

It was my distinct pleasure to prepare the candy bags for these dinners. I would stuff as much candy as I could fit into them because I wanted to do a good job. Someone would eventually tell me, "That's too much. Take some out." And I'd think to myself, *Why?* To me, more seemed better.

It was disappointing because I thought I was doing something good. But I went on and did what they said, took some out, and that's when I saw it was actually easier to close the bags.

It wasn't that more wasn't better—it was that sometimes less is better, depending on what the container can hold to be secured properly.

How many times have you thought to yourself, *If I could have a little more time, or get a little more money, then I'll be satisfied*? The world we live in depicts "more" as better—more money, more house, more cars, more jewelry, more clothes, more love, more fame, or even more social media followers. We strive to get more of everything except God. We think once we are saved, that's it. But there is more to God than Him giving us His Son, Jesus, for salvation.

We could spend our entire lives learning about Him and still die without having experienced all there is to know of Him.

In our limited time on earth, how could we possibly grasp the complexities of a God who spoke and the world came into being? A God whose very presence was too powerful for man to look upon. A God who said, "For my thoughts are not your thoughts, neither are your ways my ways" (Isaiah 55:8, NIV). A God who *is* eternity. It will take eternity itself for any human to fully know Him—and the more we know of Him, the more we learn about ourselves.

Although I still desire nice things—a multi-generational home where I can care for my aging parents and have all my bills paid—more than this, I desire God. My prayer has become, "Lord, increase my capacity for You. Make room in me to handle more of You." I must decrease so that He can increase. More of Him and less of me. Because for us to truly grow in the things of God, we must realize, as Paul said in Romans 7:18 (KJV): "For I know that in me (that is, in my flesh) dwelleth no good thing." As long as we tend to the flesh more than we do the Spirit of God, we are going to be in a constant battle—going back and forth between God's way and our way.

Consider Galatians 5:17-18 (NLT):

The sinful nature wants to do evil, which is just the opposite of what the Spirit wants. And the Spirit gives us desires that are the opposite of what the sinful nature desires. These two are constantly fighting each other, so you are not free to carry out your good intentions.

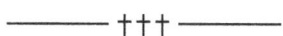

Complete surrender to God is what He wants from us—not just half of us, because the half we usually give is the part that follows the path of least resistance. When we fully surrender, then He can fully be God in our lives and show us more than we could ever imagine.

Now unto Him who is able to do exceedingly, abundantly above all that we ask or think, according to the power that works in us. (Ephesians 3:20, KJV)

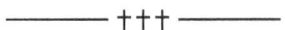

Music became a part of my life when I was 12 years old. Because I spent so much time at the church, playing around on the instruments was entertaining.

I can't believe I'm admitting this, but back then, we didn't have cell phones or tablets to play with. The piano was so beautiful—it almost felt as though it was calling to me, saying, *"Come play me."*

This piano was a bright white Kawai baby grand—stunning. Hitting a few keys here and there wasn't really making music, mostly just noise. One day during a practice, one of the musicians called me over to the organ and said, *"Play this."* They played a few keys, and I mimicked what they did. To my surprise, I caught on quickly. It was just in me. I don't know how I knew, but my fingers seemed to figure out what my ears heard.

From that moment on, I was trained as one of the church musicians. I mainly played for the Angel Choir, which, for those who didn't grow up in church, was the children's choir for ages 12 and under. I also sang in the choir. Someone saw something in me that I didn't see in myself. If they hadn't called me out and invested in me, I might have never discovered the gift of music on my life.

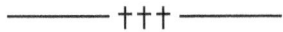

Isn't it interesting how God uses others to awaken the gifts and talents He has given us? When someone takes the time to pour into you, to teach and train you, those lessons are invaluable. I think about how Jesus deliberately mentored the disciples. He never forced them to do anything. He was intentional and patient—for the most part. I believe He was a little aggravated with them when He said, "You faithless and corrupt people! How long must I be with you? How long must I put up with you? Bring the boy here to me." (Matthew 17:17, NLT)

After Jesus rebuked the devil, the disciples asked why they couldn't do it, and Jesus immediately returned to teaching them. Ultimately, Jesus invested in the disciples and in the many who would later hear and accept Him. He was preparing them for the season when they would have to do the work without Him, and not only that, but to do it greatly.

I tell you the truth, anyone who believes in me will do the same works I have done, and even greater works, because I am going to be with the Father. (John 14:12, NLT)

One of the many things Jesus modeled for us was pouring into others and investing in them. During this season of my life, Betty was a mentor to me. I'm not sure if the gift would have become what it was had she not made that investment. *How has God used you to pour into someone else?*

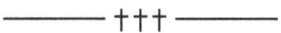

As the years went on, I learned more and more. By the time I reached middle school, my parents had enrolled me in intermediate piano classes at school a few days a week. Around that time, I had become more of a regular musician and would even accompany my pastor as she preached. I had served in nearly every area of the church that a lay member could serve, but this role was by far my favorite. I loved God. I loved to serve.

I wasn't the best musician, and often felt intimidated by the older male musicians. I practiced hard, sometimes to the point of frustration and tears, because I couldn't get certain chords right or play as well as the others.

But I gave it my all. People would say to me, "*There's something special about you. You are anointed. God's hand is on your life.*" Of course, at the time, I had no idea what those words really meant.

This is where it all started—my journey with God, from my parents' basement to a storefront church. It was where I met Him and fell in love with His presence. It was there that I was given the precious gifts of serving and the blessing of being poured into. Whether it was helping in the kitchen, filling candy bags, playing the piano for the service, ushering, or singing and directing the choir, those years became the foundational cornerstone of my life.

Those early years taught me the value of serving, but they also connected me to something deeper—a legacy of faith that ran through my family. Long before I came to understand the fullness of God for myself, I was surrounded by examples of devotion and prayer. That legacy would soon become personal, and it began with my grandmother's faith.

CHAPTER 02

The Anointing

My grandmother was a praying woman. Not only was she a prayer warrior, but she was a seer, meaning she had spiritual dreams and visions. Many people didn't understand her or believe the things she said. We were Baptist, and spiritual gifts were a challenge for this denomination to grasp back then—still is for some today. If my Granny told you something, it always came to pass. Maybe not the same day, but sure enough, people would come back to her and say that what she saw had indeed happened.

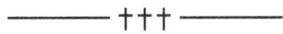

One day, during one of her many prayer sessions at home—not that she always had people over—what I call a prayer session began as her simply praying around the house. It would grow into her laying hands on me, my cousins, or whoever happened to be there at the time. One particular day I will never forget, I was between the ages of 10 and 12. She was praying and made us all start praying.

My brother and one of my cousins were there, but they retreated to their room to get out of it. My Granny was so caught up in prayer, she didn't even notice to call them back in.

My grandmother kept praying and praising God as she walked through the house, her voice rising and falling with the rhythm of her words. You could hear the steady stomp of her feet against the worn hardwood floors, the creak of the floorboards under her steps, and the occasional clap of her hands breaking through the air, exuding authority. It was intercession and spiritual warfare. She called on Jesus in that deep, soul-stirring tone only a Black grandmother could carry—part song, part declaration—letting every syllable roll out with power. Scripture spilled from her lips in between shouts of "Hallelujah!" and "Thank You, Jesus!" as she moved from room to room.

We followed behind her, praying—probably just repeating *"Thank You, Jesus"* over and over because we didn't know what else to say. As we made our way to the hallway between the bathroom and the kitchen, something suddenly swept through the house. My brother and I began to cry. My grandmother urged us to keep praising Him, to keep telling Him thank you. So, we did.

I cried *"Thank you, Jesus"* until I couldn't control the words anymore. I started jumping up and down until she came and hugged me as tight as she could. I wept in her arms. I didn't understand what was happening. I was a little scared, but I sensed it was okay—that it was good. When I opened my eyes, I saw my brother running and jumping in the kitchen, all while crying.

That was the night we were filled with the Holy Ghost.

One thing I have learned is that the Holy Spirit comes for and with a purpose. While His presence often stirs an emotional response in us—our human bodies reacting to His sheer power—His purpose is much greater than an emotional high. Of course, as a child, I had no idea what was happening. It scared me at times, but something deep inside me was connected to this presence I was feeling.

There was a song they gave me to lead at church entitled *My God Can Do It All*. I have no idea where this song came from or if our choir leaders made it up.

The verse went like this:

If you have a problem you can't solve, maybe your situation cannot be resolved, stop complaining, start believing, there's nothing too hard for God. If God can't do it, it can't be done.

Then the vamp—choir people know what this is—went like this:

Lord, do it.

We repeated it over and over. As the choir sang, I would ad-lib, probably because I was told to, "Even though I'm just a little girl, help me to live the way You want me to live."

One time when I sang this, I closed my eyes and felt something happening. I kept repeating, "*Help me to live, help me to live, the way You want me to live. Lord, do it. Lord, do it.*" When I opened my eyes, I saw people weeping, hands lifted, others crying out in worship. I didn't know exactly what was happening, but I couldn't stop singing. I just kept going until I was crying myself. I looked at my grandmother sitting in the front row—she was in full-blown worship. She stood up, came to me, and held me tight. It felt like all the strength had left my body.

The church erupted in praise, shouting, and dancing. God did something that day while my grandmother prayed, holding me in her arms.

It was strange, but in that moment I understood—*He heard me.* All I really wanted was for God to help me live how He wanted me to live.

There was something different about me. I was changed. Explaining supernatural encounters is very challenging. Human language is incapable of fully articulating the power of God. It's one of those things you have to experience for yourself.

I find myself with the same difficulties our grandparents and great-grandparents faced when trying to explain it. That's why some of the lyrics and descriptions they used were things like:

It's like fire shut up in my bones.

Something got a hold of me.

He touched me; oh, the joy that floods my soul.

Something happened, and now I know.

I looked at my hands, and they looked new. I looked at my feet, and they did too.

After this divine encounter, I felt different on the inside. I was more conscious, with a heightened sense of knowing. There was an awareness within me that I had never experienced before.

I didn't seem to fit in with the other kids. I had very few friends my age and was almost always the youngest in the room. My cousins, who were eight to ten years older than I, would confide in me, sharing their problems. I mostly listened, but occasionally I would share my thoughts.

I think I had a pretty normal childhood. I was blessed to have both parents in the home who raised my brother and me in the fear of the Lord—and with the belt. People would say, "She's anointed." But what did that really mean? All I knew was that I loved this God I had connected with, and wanted to live my life to please Him—and I still do.

This girl, who loved God and His church, had dreams for her life. They weren't complicated or outrageous—just simple. I dreamed of having a happy little family, a beautiful house, and a career. I wanted to raise my family and live happily ever after. But little did I know, things wouldn't be as simple as I thought.

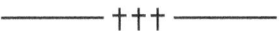

Here's something you should know about being anointed: when you are anointed, you are an automatic target for the enemy. Why? Because it is the anointing that destroys yokes.

Isaiah 10:27 (KJV) says:

And it shall come to pass in that day, that his burden shall be taken away from off thy shoulder, and his yoke shall be destroyed because of the anointing.

I define being anointed as possessing a spiritual empowerment by God, ignited by the Holy Spirit for His cause—to promote positive change in the lives of those who experience it. We must understand that when the Lord anoints you, it is not for you—it's for the Kingdom. The Kingdom of God, simply put, is God's way of doing things. People who boast about their "anointing" are not carrying the anointing of God. The anointing of God costs you something, and that cost will humble you.

People who brag and boast may have charisma, but the real anointing doesn't boast in itself. Paul says in 2 Corinthians 4:7 (KJV), "But we have this treasure in earthen vessels, that the excellency of the power may be of God, and not us." And if people allow pride, arrogance, and sin into their lives, God can and will remove His anointing from them.

We see this in the life of King Saul in 1 Samuel 15 and 16—when sin entered, God removed His anointing. Saul's disobedience left him trying to operate in an anointing that was no longer there, and it didn't work. The enemy's goal is to get you to sin, to doubt, and to do anything that will cause you to forfeit the anointing God placed on your life. John 10:10 (NLT) says, "The thief's purpose is to steal and kill and destroy. My purpose is to give them a rich and satisfying life."

I often say, the enemy doesn't care about your house, your job, your car, or your money—he is after what's in you. But he will use those very things that matter to you to manipulate and discourage you. The enemy knows that what's in you is greater and more valuable than anything outside of you. As 1 John 4:4 (KJV) says, "Ye are of God, little children, and have overcome them: because greater is He that is in you, than he that is in the world."

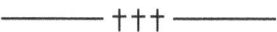

I want to encourage and remind you—there is greatness inside of you, and it is far more precious than anything you can see with your natural eyes.

The Bible says it this way:

We now have this light shining in our hearts, but we ourselves are like fragile clay jars containing this great treasure. This makes it clear that the inner power we have is from God, not from ourselves. We are pressed on every side by troubles, but we are not crushed. We are perplexed, but not driven to despair. We are hunted down, but never abandoned by God. We get knocked down, but we are not destroyed (2 Corinthians 4:7-9, NLT).

This is a powerful truth—when you understand the value of what you carry, you'll understand the attack on your life. You, my dear, are a treasure carrier. Understand this: God knew from the beginning who He was entrusting this treasure to. He knew we're fragile like clay, but He gave it to us anyway! We get to carry the precious gift of the Holy Ghost and the powerful Word of God.

God trusts us with this treasure. Even in our brokenness, in spite of our mistakes and our despair, it remains. That's why Paul said (and I'm paraphrasing) in 2 Corinthians 4:7-9, troubles will come on every side—but we will not be crushed. You may feel the pressure of life, but it will not destroy you. We are perplexed—completely baffled and puzzled—but not in despair. Have you ever felt completely baffled? I know I have, and confused. And, even though we may feel distressed, we won't become it.

God will not allow trouble to consume us. He says we will be persecuted—to be subject to hostility, harassment, or annoyance—and the enemy often uses people to do it. But you will not be forsaken. God has not forgotten you. He will come through. For He has said, "I will never leave thee, nor forsake thee." (Hebrews 13:5, KJV)

We may get knocked down, but we will not be destroyed. We will get back up again—still carrying the treasure. The answer to what it means to be anointed was revealed to me over time. It wasn't something I initially asked for—it was a gift from God.

But, being anointed comes with a price—a cost you don't

always see coming and one that you are not always willing to pay. It's not a title you wear; it's a life you live. I didn't fully understand that when I received the Holy Ghost as a young girl. I only knew that God's presence was real and that He was calling me to something greater.

Over time, I learned that with the anointing came responsibility, sacrifice, and moments of deep testing. The target on my back wasn't imaginary—it was real, and it followed me into every season of my life. What I once saw as the favor of God, I began to realize came with its own set of challenges. And those challenges…they would soon test everything I thought I knew about God, about myself, and about the life I dreamed of living. The weight of that calling often collided with the dreams I was holding onto, forcing me to question what was real and what was only imagined.

CHAPTER 03

Favor vs. Fantasy

Once I thought life could be a fairytale—a world I had created for myself because I loved God, and I knew He loved me back. However, thinking that God would give me everything I prayed for was not a wrong belief, but it was definitely a misguided one. I thought if I just prayed for something, it would come to pass. My faith was just that strong. Up until this point, there was nothing I had asked God for that I did not receive. He loved and provided for me, so why would He change now? This stage was what I like to call selfish faith—it was all about what I wanted, when I wanted it. Maybe God was using my desires to establish my trust in Him. The things I prayed for, even though they weren't major, always came to pass. I truly felt like God favored me, and for a while, that was enough.

———— ††† ————

The Bible says in Romans 1:17 (KJV), "For therein is the righteousness of God revealed from faith to faith: as it is written,

The just shall live by faith." As we grow in the Word of God and mature in the things of God, we should also grow in faith. Here is a good way to gauge your level of faith: when you reach the point where you can believe and trust God for the things He wants for your life, rather than just the things you want, you have moved from selfish faith to a more mature faith.

Most often, our flesh is not readily receptive to what God wants for us. What He desires is usually contrary to everything that pleases the flesh. Our faith has to be built on the Word of God, not in the "stuff" we ask Him for. When we don't get the job, the promotion, the house, the car, the man, or the woman—or when God doesn't do things the way we want—can we still believe?

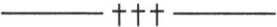

I spent a lot of time at my grandmother's house. She was the only grandmother I had the opportunity to know. My maternal grandmother passed away when my mom was only sixteen years old. I wish I had met her and learned about the other side of my family, but her life was cut short by cancer. Her name was Leona. From the pictures I've seen of her, she was very beautiful, very classy-looking—a lot like my mom.

Throughout my life, I've grieved her death without ever meeting her because I've always felt as if something was missing. There are things about me that only she could explain. I wonder what it would be like to hear the sound of her voice, to feel her embrace. I'm still curious to know what about me resembles her the most. How would I have been impacted if I had my maternal grandmother in my life? I don't know. But not having that opportunity left a mark on me.

I loved spending summers at my grandmother's house. My cousins and I would play outside all day. I was the one she would call on to pick the switches for my cousins. I can't remember her ever whooping me. I really think I was her favorite.

I was a tree climber, and at my grandma's, there was a beautiful plum tree in the front yard. My cousins and I would climb it and eat the plums straight from the branches, their juice bursting in our mouths—not sweet, but bitter, maybe because they weren't ripe yet. Still, it was a taste I'll never forget.

Not only did I climb trees, but I'd also climb on top of Granny's garage. Why? I don't know—probably because I was doing what the other kids did. We'd climb to the top, and I'd stand there like I was queen of the world before jumping off. Probably not the smartest thing to do, but I did it anyway. I'm sure we kept our angels busy at work.

As I mentioned before, I often felt out of place as a young girl. I didn't fit in with the other kids, and I wasn't able to participate in many of the things they did because I had to be at church. I learned the value of responsibility at an early age. I was expected to attend every rehearsal and church service because of my position. Even when my pastor preached out of town, I was there serving.

The funny thing is that I loved it—and sometimes despised it—at the same time. There were moments when I complained to myself and didn't want to serve in the capacity that was expected of me. But I was afraid of disappointing people and God. I wanted to please everyone and make them proud. I would think to myself, *Why do I always have to do this? Can't somebody else do it? I want to be like everybody else. Why do people expect so much from me anyway?* I had to be responsible even when I wanted to be irresponsible. I didn't want to be destructive or disobedient; I just wanted the freedom not to show up sometimes.

My pastor and the other leaders didn't make it easy for me at church. They were tough. If I weren't playing with the right spirit or in the way my pastor wanted, she would openly rebuke me during service. I would be so embarrassed, sitting there playing with tears rolling down my face. I remember one Sunday morning, I was playing for her as she was closing out her sermon. The spirit was high, but my pastor seemed as if something was bothering her. She looked over at me in frustration. Maybe I wasn't playing the right chords, or perhaps I was disrupting her flow during preaching. Whatever it was, she stopped her sermon, turned toward me, and said over the microphone, *"That's not right. If you are going to play, play right!"*

I didn't know then that these moments were lessons—teaching me how to receive correction and not carry my feelings on my shoulders. It toughened me up, and it also made me want to give my best and serve with a spirit of excellence.

In the years to come, many of the girls I grew up with in church began getting married. They had beautiful weddings and married seemingly wonderful men. Most of the time, I was the musician for their ceremonies. I dreamed of the day when I would have my own wedding and marry my wonderful man. It felt like it was taking forever. This is how it usually went for me: the men I was interested in weren't interested in me, and the men interested in me weren't the ones I wanted. I wanted my happily ever after, too—because that's what I thought happiness was.

Life has an interesting way of teaching you that you can't dictate what happens. Believing that, because I loved God, everything in life would go exactly as I wanted was a fairy tale in itself.

———— ††† ————

After graduating from high school, I was excited about my future. I enrolled in college and looked forward to the experience. I had considered a few career paths, but I ultimately chose nursing. I wanted to help people. That felt like the Christian thing to do, but beyond that, it genuinely gave me fulfillment.

Toward the end of my second semester, the Nursing Program Director called to discuss my progress. I thought I was doing reasonably well. Labs were fun and easy, and I caught on quickly. But I struggled with test-taking. No matter how much I studied, I found myself nervous. I would overthink answers, use all the allotted time, and still fail. Back then, I couldn't figure out why. Reviewing the tests later, I realized I had known many of the correct answers but had changed them. I didn't realize at the time that what I was experiencing was test anxiety.

During our meeting, the Director suggested I consider switching majors, implying that maybe nursing wasn't the right fit for me. I believed her and trusted her judgment. *Surely, if the head of the program thought that, it must be true.* I needed to keep a C average to stay in the program, but my last test earned me a D, putting my place in the program at risk. I was devastated and felt like a total failure.

I sat in my dull gray 1980 Mercury Lynx, a small, boxy hatchback with faded paint that seemed to match the cold December gloom, crying and asking God what I was supposed to do with my life. After a week of thinking and talking with my parents, I decided to withdraw from college before the next semester started. I didn't feel smart enough to continue. My parents warned me not to stop, saying it would be hard to go back. Maybe they knew something I didn't. However, grounded in my independence, I wanted to figure out my path.

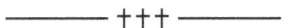

Working became my next attempt at independence. So, I took a part-time job as a janitor at the mall. That didn't last long—because mall bathrooms are disgusting. After that, I worked with a temp agency, packing supplies at a factory, filling boxes as they moved down the conveyor belt. It lasted two weeks. I quickly realized that wasn't God's plan for my life. I returned to the agency, and they found me a more promising position. Someone there knew my pastor and recommended me for a job with a company contracted by the city to collect citations—one more suited to who I was as a person.

I was the smiling face behind the counter where people came to pay for parking and municipal violations. Most people weren't happy to see me, but I greeted them kindly. Within months, I was promoted to lead cashier. I started to feel good about myself again.

It was a beautiful, sunny day. I was at work when a man walked in, placed a dozen long-stemmed red roses on the counter, and quickly slipped out the door. I froze, stunned—I had never experienced anything like this before. For a moment, I just stared, captivated by how beautiful they were, with their deep red petals opening softly and the fragrant scent filling the area. But curiosity quickly took over. *Who are these from? Who was this guy? Why did he run out like that?*

I searched for the card, my fingers trembling slightly as I opened it. The note read something like, I have admired you for some time and had to let you know how I felt. My heart skipped—not with excitement, but from uncertainty. He was a young man from church who had visited us before, but I didn't know him.

As a young woman in church, I'd had men tell me they heard "god" (notice I said with a little *g*) say I was their wife. My response was always, "When He tells me, I'll let you know." This one was no different.

However, over time, I realized this man was strategic. He befriended my grandmother, mother, and pastor. Eventually, through his persistence, I agreed to go out with him. I hadn't dated much, so this was a new experience for me.

At first, I completely dismissed him, rarely giving him a second thought. But over time, that same persistence began to break down my hesitance. Every thoughtful gesture, kind word, and moment we shared seemed to soften the walls I had built. As we went out more often, I started to enjoy his company. He was charming, funny, and easy to be around. Gradually, I began to see him differently—not just as that young man from church, but as someone who made me laugh, listened to me when I spoke, and appeared genuinely interested in who I was.

One day, I found myself wondering if this could be the very thing I had dreamed of as a little girl. *Could he be the answer to my childhood prayer? My fairy tale? My "Prince Charming"—the man I had imagined walking beside, like the couples I had watched growing up?* I didn't have the answer yet, but something inside me was stirring, and I knew I'd soon find out.

CHAPTER 04

My Dreams Come True

Getting to know my newfound "Prince Charming" started off great. We talked every day and saw each other several times a week. It was during this time that I learned he was a pastor. At first, I was fine with it, thinking, *What harm could it cause?* After all, we were getting to know each other. But time moved quickly with us, and within a month or so, we were pretty much inseparable.

I started dreaming about what a possible future with this man might look like. My dreams were wonderful. I imagined my house, my white picket fence, my children, and him as my husband and best friend. Maybe I was trying to imitate what I saw in my parents' marriage. As a child, I saw my Mom and Dad loving each other and building a life together.

Early on, they both worked. My mom still managed to make our house feel like a home and took care of us. My Dad provided for us, mowed the lawn, and fixed things around the house. They would talk and laugh a lot, especially when they'd watch *Fred Sanford* or

The Jeffersons. Things weren't always easy, but I watched them get through many tough times together.

Although life was busy, they made time to rest and spend moments together as a family. I remember our road trips. For some reason, back then, we would dress up to get in the car for hours of riding, and my Mom and Dad would wear matching outfits. I think it was mostly my Mom's idea, but Dad always went along with it.

Strangely enough, they still do that today. The example my parents set had a big impact on how I viewed marriage. I saw the potential in who I believed he could be, and the potential of who I thought I could become with him. I envisioned this wonderful life. Even though I wasn't thrilled about being a pastor's wife, I told myself that it would at least be an opportunity to help people. I thought, *maybe this is God's plan*.

Once that image was engraved in my mind and spirit, I threw myself into hoping and praying it would happen. Everything seemed to be falling into place just as I had imagined. Then it happened—six months into dating, he asked me to marry him. Although I had dreamed of this moment, I never expected it to happen so soon.

When he popped the question, my stomach turned. I was nervous—and in true church fashion, it couldn't be simple. He proposed at one of his pastoral banquets, in front of all those people.

There were people from all over the city and out of town. Friends, church members, other pastors from churches he fellowshipped with, his parents, siblings, cousins, and even my family. They were all at this banquet. I was put on the spot. Even though I thought this was what I wanted, I still felt a little afraid. When it happened, people came and took me from my seat and sat me in a chair in the middle of the room. He stood in front of me, then slowly lowered himself onto one knee, opening a small box to reveal a ring, and asked the question I had always longed to hear: "*Will you marry me?*" With my knots in my stomach, I said, "*Yes!*" In that moment, it was magical. But there was one thing that lingered.

On the way home, for a brief moment, I wondered if I had made the right decision. I kept looking down at the ring on my finger as thoughts flooded my mind: *Should I marry him? Maybe I should tell him now—or maybe not?* But the moment passed. This was my friend. I loved him. He treated me as if I were the most precious thing on earth. This was going to be my dream come true. This was really happening.

I guess I thought faith meant creating an image in your mind and hoping it would come true. In all my dreaming, I never really considered what it would be like to have a husband who was pastoring or what that would entail for me. I was in love with him, and I believed that was all I needed.

The ministry, although good, wasn't my main focus. I figured everything would fall into place, and we would live happily ever after in our house with the white picket fence. I would soon learn some valuable lessons.

Potential can be wonderful, even when it's only imagined. By definition, potential means having or showing the capacity to become or develop into something in the future. That can be admirable, but you shouldn't marry someone because of it. A person with potential has the capacity to develop into many different things, but there's no guarantee what that will be. You have to enter marriage being content with who they are at that moment, because that may be all they will ever want to be—and you have to be okay with that.

One issue with potential is that you can only control the potential within yourself. You cannot control someone else's. Potential may go unrealized or never be reached. You cannot build anything on potential alone. It cannot serve as the foundation of a relationship. If your relationship is based on potential, you'll constantly look for the person to change. And if they are not making progress as you expect, you might take it personally—thinking they don't love you enough to change—or you may begin to feel you aren't worth the effort.

Untapped potential can cause disappointment. A disappointed wife might become a nag or withdraw emotionally. Either way, it's harmful to a relationship. Disappointment is like poison to a marriage, especially if the foundation is already fragile.

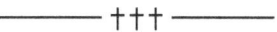

Looking back, I realize I envisioned the potential of who I wanted him to be. Maybe I believed that if a husband could be sanctified by his wife, he could also be transformed by her. But I learned that you cannot change another person. No matter how good your intentions are, people will only change if they want to.

Almost immediately, events began to unfold that caught me off guard. My naivety turned out to be my worst enemy. I used to believe most people were honest and that if they said something, it was true. Until then, I took everything literally—and I still do.

Don't do that. Just be direct. If I'm talking to you, I shouldn't have to decode your words like a puzzle. Say what you mean, and mean what you say.

Even with the best intentions, people say and promise things they simply can't deliver. As authentic and transparent as I thought I was, there were still parts of me I kept hidden—things I didn't want him to see. I didn't want him to see how insecure I really was.

I had always wanted to be a wife, but I wasn't completely sure I knew how, and questions kept flooding my mind because of it. Could I meet his expectations while also trying to figure out my own? I was still trying to decide what I wanted to do for a living.

What if he didn't agree with it? What if who I truly was didn't fit the mold? What if it turned out I wasn't who he thought I was? Would he still love me?

These questions added extra pressure to our future marriage. I thought I could see all of him while hiding parts of myself. In doing so, I was unintentionally deceptive, but I was also deceived. Maybe this is true for most people when dating—you're dating the version of the person they want you to see, not necessarily who they truly are.

That's why it's so important to take the time to get to know someone before even considering marriage.

Most people in their early twenties are still figuring out who they are. By the time you reach your mid to late twenties, you start to have a clearer idea of who you want to become. This was true for me. I was young and facing the same challenges. I didn't have everything figured out or know all the details about who I wanted to be, but being educated in my chosen career path was important to me. Overall, I wanted to be successful.

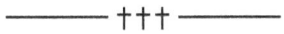

At twenty-one, I married my best friend—or at least the person I thought was my best friend. I became a wife and the First Lady of a church. Personally, I didn't know who I was, and spiritually, I didn't know either. I was becoming. In the process of learning the person God created me to be, I had a label for which I had no substantial context.

I didn't have a model of what a First Lady was exactly supposed to be like. *What did that title actually consist of? Did it mean dressing fashionably and wearing hats? That would be problematic because I did not like to wear hats.* I was lacking the wherewithal to confidently function in this new role.

Just a year earlier, I had dropped out of college. I was still lost, confused, and frustrated. Maybe that's why I felt this was the path I was meant to take. I prayed about it—or maybe I just said words to God without waiting for an answer. Perhaps I simply asked, then thanked Him for letting me have my way.

I didn't take the time to see if it was a good idea or give Him time to tell me. I rushed into marriage a few months later.

I wanted to hurry up and "start my life," even though I wasn't exactly sure why I was in such a rush. I just wanted to be independent as an adult—having my own house and building my own family. My parents suggested I wait, but I didn't listen. A few weeks after the proposal, we had already picked a wedding date, which was six months away.

Before we got married, I told my parents what we were planning, and they were a little worried. At first, there was silence; they both looked thoughtful, as if they were trying to figure out the right way to tell me that it wasn't a good idea.

First, my mom said very carefully, *"Don't you think that is too soon? You should wait a little longer."* My dad agreed with her in his way, saying, *"Yeah, I think y'all should wait."*

Looking back, I realize how selfish I was. I didn't consider their feelings at all. I had no idea what their financial situation was at the time or anything.

After I gave all my reasons, they knew I had made up my mind. I was young, and like most young people who haven't fully experienced life, I wanted what I wanted, and I went ahead—because what I wanted was a good thing, and I didn't think anything could be wrong with that.

And so, the journey began. About three months into the marriage, I found out I was pregnant. I was scared but also excited. I had no idea what to expect. In fact, even before I knew I was pregnant, I started feeling queasy off and on throughout the day.

I didn't think much of it at first—just assumed I had an upset stomach. Wanting quick relief, I reached for the only remedy I knew, a dose of bright pink Pepto-Bismol. I lay there, waiting for it to work, convinced it would settle my stomach the way it always did. Of course, it didn't. The queasiness persisted, and little did I know it wasn't just a simple stomach bug—it was the very first sign that my life was about to change forever. Don't judge me; I was just twenty-one. I even went to the ER because I felt so terrible, and that's when the doctors confirmed I was pregnant.

I was sitting impatiently on the exam table in a hospital gown, feeling terrible, wondering what was taking them so long. After what seemed like hours, the doctor finally entered and gave us the news. I sat there, eyes wide open, stunned. Following my initial reaction, a flood of emotions hit me like a wave—happy, scared, excited, nervous, overjoyed—all at the same time.

I couldn't believe there was a little human being growing inside me. I will never forget the first time I heard that tiny heartbeat. Words can't explain the overwhelming joy I felt. I was excited and nervous all at once. I watched my stomach every day, waiting to see the progress of my little baby growing.

CHAPTER 05

A Dream Lost

This was my twelve-week appointment. My doctor, following her normal procedure, went to listen for the baby's heartbeat, but she had trouble finding it. I watched her face for clues, searching for a flicker of reassurance, but her expression stayed neutral—too neutral. They immediately sent me to the ultrasound room to see exactly what was going on.

A swirl of emotions overwhelmed me as I lay back on the table, my hands gripping the thin paper beneath me. The gel felt cold against my stomach. My eyes were fixed on the black-and-white monitor, waiting for that flicker, that rhythmic flutter I'd seen in pictures and imagined so many times.

I saw the tiny hands, the little feet, the small head.

My baby was still—far too still.

In that moment, the room seemed unnaturally quiet, apart from the low hum of the machine and the faint buzz of the fluorescent lights overhead.

As the doctor gently pressed the probe and moved it from side to side, I held my breath. I was waiting to hear the steady thump-thump-thump of life at any moment.

But there was only silence.

A gut-wrenching silence.

It felt like the longer it lasted, the heavier it became.

Finally, the doctor spoke in a quiet voice and said, *"There's no heartbeat."*

In my heart, I immediately began praying, *"Lord, please let my baby's heart start beating again. Please."*

They examined my baby carefully. It felt like I was on that table for hours, although I'm sure it was only 20 minutes. My eyes never left the monitor. I thought, This is enough time for a miracle. But no rhythmic sound came. There was no small flashing on the screen to signal life. I couldn't believe this. My baby was gone.

I couldn't wrap my mind around it. This was my first baby; surely God wouldn't allow this to happen.

They sent me home to see if the baby would pass naturally, but how was I supposed to just… wait? I walked out of that hospital feeling numb, my body still carrying life that was no longer living. Every step to the car felt heavier, as if my heart was dragging behind me. I kept thinking, Maybe they're wrong. Maybe something will change. With every cramp, every still moment in my belly, I whispered under my breath, *Okay God… here's Your moment to work a miracle.*

Three days went by, and I was cramping badly, but the baby still hadn't passed. My doctor scheduled a dilation and curettage (D&C) for the next day. I felt like I was in a fog. My baby was gone—what did I do wrong? My thoughts raced, and all I could think was that God hadn't answered my prayer. My husband was mostly silent. He tried to comfort me, but I could tell he was struggling to process it himself.

Before the procedure, they did one last ultrasound. I stared at the monitor as hard as I could, trying to memorize every detail so I would never forget. My heart was shattered. It felt like the weight of the world had settled on my chest, making it hard to breathe.

I didn't cry immediately; I couldn't. My mind struggled to process the agony my body was experiencing. As they rolled me down the halls toward the operating room, I was very afraid. I'd never had any kind of operation before. The room was cold and sterile, and everyone was busy getting things set up. As they put the oxygen mask on me, my doctor knew I was overwhelmed with emotion. As the anesthesiologist told me to begin counting to 10, she told me, "Everything is going to be okay." When I woke, I could immediately tell—we were separated. My baby was gone. All I could do was weep. I cried and cried. I'd never felt heartbreak like that before.

My doctor, a sweetheart, tried to reassure me that I didn't do anything wrong and that sometimes these things just happen. She couldn't give me a reason or cause. But I wanted to know why—not just the natural why, but the spiritual one too. Up until this moment, God had always answered my prayers. Why not this time?

I went home and slept the rest of the day. The next day, I wandered around in a daze. Alone at home, I looked at the ultrasound picture and started to cry. I could hardly breathe; I gasped for air so hard it scared me. I sank to my knees, my heart pounding.

Finally able to breathe again, I sobbed uncontrollably. I had no answers. Was it something I could have done differently? I had prayed.

Over time, I learned to accept what God had permitted. I didn't understand why I had to go through this, but I accepted it. This wasn't the ideal way to start a marriage, but it was our reality. We did our best to manage. With the congregation watching, it was back to business as usual, so I adjusted in my own way.

CHAPTER 06

Dreams Attacked

It was six months later, and we were pregnant again with my first daughter. I was nervous, but each day I remained pregnant, I whispered, *Thank you, God.* I was so sick that I had to be hospitalized multiple times for dehydration because I couldn't keep anything down. My doctor diagnosed me with hyperemesis gravidarum—a severe form of morning sickness. My husband tried to stay positive, but I was miserable.

After about five months of being pregnant, the "morning" sickness—which had really been all-day sickness—began to subside, and I could finally enjoy my pregnancy.

One day, during a work meeting, I started feeling sick. My boss noticed and told me to go to the hospital.

I thought to myself, this had to be the enemy attacking my body again. I had just delivered my first message on Mother's Day. I remember it well—it was 1997, and the church was packed, with many people eager to hear me speak.

Back then, it was customary for the Pastor's wife to deliver the message on Mother's Day. At that time, my husband pretty much insisted that I do it. I really didn't want to, and I didn't think I was capable.

I don't even remember what I talked about, but while I was speaking, my voice shaking, something was happening inside me that I can't explain. Could it be that all this turmoil and trouble were meant to stir this awakening in me?

Maybe the enemy knew something I didn't know, or he could sense what God was doing. I believe that the enemy can sense a move of God.

The enemy knows when the anointing is on someone's life because he used to be that. He knows what it's like to be in God's presence. He knows what that looks like, sounds like, and smells like. The enemy can smell the oil (the anointing). His agenda is to keep people separated from God so they cannot experience the oil. Why? Because the anointing destroys yokes.

What is a yoke? In biblical times, a yoke was a wooden device used to control animals, like oxen, keeping them bound together at the neck while plowing fields or doing whatever they needed to do simultaneously. Spiritually, a "yoke" represents anything that restricts you or keeps you bound—subject to move under someone else's command—preventing freedom, growth, or destiny: spiritual, physical, or emotional bondage and oppression.

I think there are many things the enemy uses to deter, distract, and destroy destinies.

Now, if you are not familiar with the term "the enemy," it refers to Satan. I Peter 5:8 (KJV) says, "Be sober, be vigilant, because your adversary the devil, as a roaring lion, walketh about, seeking whom he may devour."

He definitely didn't want me to succeed because God was doing so much for me—a pregnancy, growth in ministry, and living my dream. That's how the devil is, though; he uses the things that are closest to us in an attempt to destroy us. This book is not a study on who the devil is or to bring any glory to him. It is, however, my goal to make someone aware of the tactics he uses.

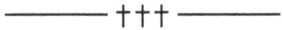

After realizing my boss was right, I went to the hospital. When I arrived, the midwife on duty monitored me and found I was contracting every five minutes. My water bag had a small leak, so I had to be admitted. They started me on magnesium sulfate to stop the contractions. I stayed in the hospital for a while. Just like clockwork, the nurses came into my room to give me medication to prevent my contractions from restarting.

Each time, the medication relaxed my entire body, even my eyes, and I could barely see most days. I stayed in bed for two weeks. I didn't mind; I just wanted my baby to be okay.

Leading up to the third week in the hospital, the doctors noticed that my baby's heart rate was fluctuating and wouldn't stabilize. We needed to deliver her immediately. They stopped the magnesium right away, hoping that labor would start naturally, but I think the prolonged use of magnesium delayed it. We either needed to try to jump-start the contractions or perform an emergency C-section. I chose to try Pitocin in hopes of a natural delivery. After some time, things regulated.

About a year after I lost my first baby, God blessed me with a beautiful baby girl. When I heard the sound of her little voice crying,

I was enamored. All ten tiny fingers and toes were accounted for. She was considered a preemie, weighing just over four pounds. She had the cutest little chubby cheeks and a silky-soft head of hair—she was perfect. Though she was a month and a half early, she arrived right on time for God's plan. After three weeks in the hospital, we brought her home. She became my life. I was determined to be the best mother I could be.

But about seven months later, one day I noticed something was wrong. Earlier that day, I had planned to go to the nail salon. It was a casual routine, so I got my daughter ready as I normally would. However, this time, I noticed her soft spot looked slightly swollen. Even though she was smiling and responsive, I told myself I'd keep an eye on it. I took her to my mom and returned an hour later. I checked her soft spot and saw it was more swollen than before. My mom urged me to call the doctor. By the time we arrived, her condition had worsened. The doctor immediately sent us to Children's Hospital, telling us to go straight there.

When we arrived, they took us straight back to the room. The pediatrician had called ahead, so they were expecting us. I barely had time to kiss my baby's forehead before they gently but firmly lifted her from my arms and laid her on the small hospital bed.

I stood at the foot of the bed, my hands gripping the cold metal rail, watching helplessly as nurse after nurse, doctor after doctor, surrounded her.

She lay there perfectly still, her chest rising and falling so slowly it terrified me. No reflexes. No movement. No sound. Not even a whimper. The silence was deafening.

They prepared her for a spinal tap. I watched as they turned her on her side, her little knees tucked in, her body looking incredibly small against the large hands of the doctor. The needle they held looked huge—so wrong—beside her tiny frame. I wanted to scream, to scoop her up and run, but my feet wouldn't move.

Inside, I was falling apart, but I forced myself to stay upright. I had to be strong for my baby. My eyes burned as I blinked away tears, not wanting them to see me break down. I kept asking, "Is she going to be okay?" No one answered at first. The silence was worse than any words could have been.

Finally, a nurse looked up briefly and said softly, *"She's a very sick little girl."*

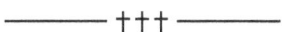

The words echoed in my ears. I felt sick to my stomach. I looked at her father, seeking strength, but his face reflected my fear—hollow eyes, lips pressed tight, trying not to fall apart. Then, he broke down, tears flowing down his cheeks. I reached for him, but inside I felt even more alone because I needed him to be strong for both of us.

When they finally finished, I stood frozen, my eyes locked on the monitors. The steady beeps and blinking lines had become my lifeline—every sound and flicker assuring me my baby was still here. But I knew we were in a fight, and I didn't know how it would turn out.

The results came back: spinal meningitis. I had just heard about it months earlier on the news when it took the life of a young child. Now my baby was fighting it. She was admitted for aggressive treatment. Doctors warned us about possible side effects if she survived. I stayed by her side, praying constantly.

After a week, she started to get better. The swelling went down. She was responsive again. My heart could breathe.

When I went back to church that Sunday during the service, I sat at the organ and started singing this song:

Lord, you know that I'm your child,
And I'm doing the best that I can.
Why my way gets so dark,
You know I just don't understand.
Oh Lord, I need You to hold my hand,
I can't make it without You Lord.

At this point in my life, I really couldn't understand why God would allow these kinds of things to happen. After three weeks, she was discharged. God had healed her. Many people had died that year from the same illness, but God spared her life.

Over twenty years later, I still give Him praise for it.

CHAPTER 07

A Dream Disturbed

Looking back I see how the enemy used fear to try to destroy me. As a child, I was sensitive to spiritual things. I often had dreams and experienced what is scientifically called sleep paralysis. I would struggle in my sleep—sometimes wanting to wake up from a frightening dream but unable to, or waking up with the sensation that something heavy was sitting on me. I couldn't move or scream. I was afraid and deeply fearful of evil spirits.

I was terrified of movies that involved demonic activity. I remember when *The Exorcist* came out; I was so shaken by it. I didn't understand why the priest couldn't control the demon spirit. In church, I had already seen demons being cast out, which was frightening enough for a child. I remember moments when demons would speak out and show themselves as they were being cast away. My experiences in church, along with what I saw in those movies, created a fear in me that I struggled with throughout my childhood.

To this day, I don't watch anything involving demonic activity—not because I'm still afraid, but because I won't play with the devil. I fought with the spirit of fear in my childhood, and it still tries to creep back in. I have to remind myself of 2 Timothy 1:7 (KJV), "For God has not given us the spirit of fear, but of power, love, and a sound mind."

The second thing the enemy used against me was the spirit of perversion. As a child, I was inappropriately touched by another child who was older than me. Perhaps they had seen things, or someone had demonstrated this behavior to them, but it was wrong. As kids often say, "Please don't tell. I don't want to get in trouble." I was startled by it and frightened, so I never said anything. As time went on, I had forgotten it even happened until fear triggered the memory. Fear had a grip on me.

Being afraid of the scary images depicting the enemy and having a misguided view of what God created to be pure set me up for the enemy's attempt to destroy God's plan for my life. I wanted to get married, raise children, grow old with my husband, have a career to earn a living, and live a normal life. At this point in my journey, I loved God, loved my husband, and was committed to supporting him and his ministry efforts.

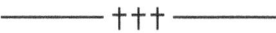

It seemed like, as time went on, the more distant we became. I never asked to do anything in the ministry, but if I saw a need, I tried to fulfill it. I'm sure that at some point I would have obeyed God, but it was his encouragement that pushed me into the preaching ministry. Although it was a hard thing to have lived through, I chose not to regret it. After things ended, I replayed the what-ifs and the shoulda, woulda, coulda in my mind. I wondered how much differently things might have turned out if I had not married him and instead focused on my education and career.

One day, the Lord told me:

Don't you regret another day the decisions you made or what you have been through, because it was there that I called you. It was in this place that I anointed you. It was in this place that you learned of Me. It was in this place that you learned to operate the gifts that I placed inside of you. Don't regret it another day.

What do you say to that? My answer: *"Yes, Lord."*

I faced many challenges, and my marriage was falling apart. One of the things I started to fear was my husband cheating on me. Most women have this thought at some point in their relationship, given the right circumstances.

Early in my marriage, I noticed other women showing interest in my husband. I didn't realize it at first, but there were even people he had been involved with before me who were still members of the church.

I felt secure at first because I had no reason to doubt where his heart was. Let's just say that after about three years of marriage, I completely understood why so many First Ladies often looked mean and seemed to have a bad attitude most of the time. Expecting to be kind and nice to people who intentionally disrespect you, speak against you, and try to tear you down and wreck your home is extremely difficult.

For me, it wasn't always outright acts of disrespect—because early on, that rarely happened—but it was the secretive, sneaky, behind-my-back stuff that really bothered me. But, as the faithful woman of God I was, I prayed. I was determined to keep my house and the church happy and joyful.

―― †††――

The church was two years old when I arrived, a very small congregation with most members under the age of 30. Although I didn't desire to be a First Lady or anything similar, I saw it as a privilege that the Lord granted me an opportunity to serve in this role. My goal was to do the Lord's will and make Him proud. I never expected it to be easy, but I certainly didn't expect it to turn out like it did.

I didn't really know what it was like to be a First Lady. I grew up with a woman Pastor. I would only see First Ladies from churches that would visit. As I mentioned earlier, most of them always seemed intimidating. *I smiled.* I had no idea what to expect—how to act, what to do, or not do. I tried to pattern myself after my husband's Pastor's wife. She was the only one I had seen up close and personal: Mrs. Dorothy Nell Sims.

I smile when I think of her. She always seemed to be smiling; she wasn't like some of the others I had seen. In my mind, she was the epitome of a Pastor's wife. She was beautiful, classy, well-spoken, and loving. She seemed to light up a room whenever she entered.

Mrs. Sims took me under her wing, loved me, and nurtured me. She handled me gently, knowing I was so naïve and had no real clue. I loved how her church seemed to genuinely love her. She spoke at a service where she officially installed me as the First Lady. Her topic was:

"Welcome to This Field of Service."

I will never forget it. It was an inspiring yet eye-opening message. Her words focused on service and opened my eyes to see a different side of the position—a servant.

First Ladies are some of the most misunderstood, unseen, and judged people in many ministries. I never understood why some women seemed to covet the title and envy the position but had no idea of the cost. Mrs. Sims introduced me to a wonderful group of women, as she was the President of the Ministers' Wives and Widows of our area. I watched her closely. She taught me many things—from never setting my purse on the floor in the sanctuary to smiling sweetly when my husband honors me from the pulpit before his sermons. She was built differently. I was different and didn't try to imitate her, but I tried to learn from her. I loved her deeply and miss her greatly.

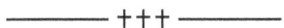

A few months into our marriage, my husband brought his little sister to stay with us. This wasn't a big problem; she was his sister and needed a place to stay. She didn't stay long, but shortly after that, he brought other kids to live with us. I wanted to help, but I wasn't included in these decisions. I was just told as they arrived, along with all the other kids who wanted to hang out at our house.

Having the kids over now and then wasn't a big deal—I enjoyed having some of them around.

It was the way decisions were made without my input and how things were handled that made me feel disrespected and uncomfortable in my own home. It made me feel robbed of creating memories with my daughter and husband. I now felt forced to stretch myself in a way I wasn't ready for. Maybe that was a selfish way for me to feel, but that's how I truly felt.

Trying to be a good wife, I went along with it, hoping things would improve. I took on most of the responsibility for cooking, getting food, transporting everyone, and taking them shopping—all while caring for a toddler. I managed, but deep inside, I felt that something wasn't quite right in my heart.

I started seeing less and less of my husband. He'd leave early and come home late. He drove to church without us, and we hardly ever rode together. But I would suppress my feelings of displeasure and carry on with life.

As time went on, I noticed that we had stopped communicating. We didn't hold conversations unless they were necessary—not because I was mad or we were at odds. I would try to talk to him and wanted him to be as interested in talking to me as he was to everyone else, but that never seemed to be the case. I started to feel like there was something wrong with me.

Why couldn't I hold my husband's attention? We had good moments, but they were fleeting and far between. My husband never seemed happy when it was just him and me—it was only if there were tons of people around. As his wife, that saddened me, not because he was a people person, but because I realized that I would never be enough for him.

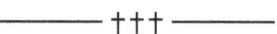

The ministry was progressing, slowly but surely. The Lord seemed to be blessing us. He would ask me to preach more often. I would resist in my spirit, and my flesh would be so nervous, but somehow every time I got up, the Lord would speak to me. I always studied and had my script, but I started hearing more in my spirit, and I learned how to just say what I heard Him say.

When the Spirit of God began to move in a service, I would find myself drawn to certain people, and God would use me to minister to them—not with many words, but sometimes with just a hug. I became more involved in organizing women's gatherings and prayer meetings. Some of the ladies and I would gather to pray in their homes, and the Spirit of God would begin to move. God healed and delivered. It always amazed me because, first of all, I was usually the youngest there, and these women trusted my leadership. Second, I knew it was not me—it was God. He was showing me who He was and teaching me who I was.

I prayed that things would get better. I never wanted to be the nagging type of wife, and I'm not a confrontational person, so many times I just didn't say much. When I did speak up, it always seemed to lead to an argument. I hated to argue. He was always so defensive. Nothing was ever resolved, and I only felt worse afterward. I honestly didn't know what to do or who I could trust to talk about it.

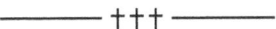

About a month after we moved into our new home, I came home from work to find my husband had brought two boys home from his job. He explained that they had been pulled out of their home suddenly as an emergency, and their social worker couldn't take them, so they had nowhere to go. The school where he worked asked if he could keep them temporarily on an emergency placement basis. I felt sorry for them and was saddened that they had to go through such a situation, which made me less focused on the fact that he hadn't discussed it with me beforehand. Besides, *I figured this would just be temporary, right?*

A few days went by, and the next thing I was told was that they would be placed in our home permanently as foster children. I felt worried. We never discussed becoming foster parents.

I was also worried because of our two-year-old daughter—how she would react to them, how this would affect her, and whether I could handle taking care of them. That was my concern. I wasn't completely against it, but my concerns weren't really considered or addressed by my husband.

They were very nice boys who were going through a tough time, and they grew on me. Initially, they spent a considerable amount of time with my husband, but after a few months, they became more of my responsibility. My husband would be gone all day and come home at night. When he came home, he would do his own little thing, and I would do mine. It became a very dangerous routine.

In the hustle and bustle of daily life, we just kept going as usual—well, I did. He would be so happy and jovial around other people, and all the while, I felt like I was dying inside. *How could he be so happy when our relationship was struggling?* I would suggest spending more time together. I would express my concern about what was happening or not happening in the marriage, but it usually went in one ear and out the other.

We never took vacations together. We didn't have date nights. All our time was spent at church.

One evening, I brought up the idea of having another child. Looking back, I don't know why—maybe I thought it might make us focus more on our family. It wasn't a long, heartfelt talk. It went more like this:

I asked, *"What do you think about having another baby?"*

He responded, *"I don't know. I haven't really thought about it."*

I said, *"It would be good to have a sibling for our daughter. She is getting older—she's five now."*

I think I was just happy to have his attention for that moment. He agreed, and we decided to have another child.

During all my pregnancies, I was sick and spent most days in bed and in the bathroom. I'm sure I wasn't much fun to be around. Most of the time, I was alone. That's why I'm so thankful for my mom. She always came in and saved the day. She went to the store, cooked for the family, cleaned—she did it all. *I definitely wouldn't have made it without her. She will forever be my hero!*

While I was on bed rest, I recall spending a lot of time praying and journaling. My relationship with God deepened during this time. I could hear Him more clearly and feel His presence more strongly for some reason. It was amazing.

I recognized this moment, and I recall the feeling I had while sitting on the bed, praying and writing in my journal—it was as if the Spirit of the Lord was breathing on me. I felt calm and peaceful. I knew He was with me. I knew He heard me. *I wanted to hold onto this feeling forever.*

Although I couldn't understand what was happening in my marriage, I committed to praying and staying. *Any day now, I was waiting for a breakthrough.*

My husband would meet all kinds of people. He was a people-person. There were some people I absolutely did not prefer. I made my feelings known, but that didn't matter to him. He would still invite them over, no matter how uncomfortable it made me. Some of them were witches—people sent straight from the pit of hell. I was in constant warfare when they were around.

I felt like he prioritized everyone else over me. The church came first, then his friends, his kids, his family, and finally me. The only place I felt like I had any worth as a wife was at church. That was where I believed he needed me. At home, I wasn't the priority, but at church, it had to be different. He had to uphold the standards of being perfect in the eyes of others. That became the place where I found my value. *It was a desperate attempt to find self-worth in a situation where I felt completely devalued and ignored in my own home life.*

The pressure to conform and look flawless within the church became *a twisted form of self-protection, a desperate cling to the illusion of acceptance and belonging* when those things were missing from my daily life.

CHAPTER 08

A Dream Turned Nightmare

By this point, I had already begun to feel the slow drift between us, but one moment stands out so clearly in my mind, almost as if it's frozen in time. We were working at the same school then, and I was walking down the hallway when my husband passed by without slowing down. He glanced at me and said, *"Why are you looking like you lost your best friend?"*

I forced a small, awkward smile, but inside, my heart sank. In that instant, *I knew—I had lost my best friend.* Something inside me shifted.

The loneliness that had been quietly building now felt like a wave that swallowed me whole. I would go to bed alone and wake up alone. On some nights, I'd catch only a glimpse of him, but even then, it felt like I was in this marriage by myself.

I remember one year I really wanted to go on vacation. I practically begged him to take me somewhere. I was determined that if he didn't want to go, I would go alone. I was six months pregnant at the time with my second daughter, and one of my friends felt sorry for me and decided she would go with me so I wouldn't be alone.

I was disappointed and hurt, but I tried to make the best of it. While on vacation, I told myself, *Tina, keep working at it.* I called my husband to talk to him, but he seemed preoccupied. I told him I loved him, and his response was, *"I'm flattered."*

What kind of response was that? I was so hurt, so tired—I knew.

About three months after I gave birth, I was home when I got a phone call. It was a young woman who sounded noticeably upset and was ranting, saying that I needed to come get my husband. If you know me, you know that I generally don't get visibly affected by most things. I told her, *"You got involved with him, you deal with it."*

I sounded amazingly calm, but I was freaking out inside. *My heart was in my throat.* She went on to say that she had been in a relationship with my husband for eight months, and she gave me details to back up her claims. I needed proof—I needed solid evidence—because there had been many other claims, but I never had physical proof. Of course, my husband would deny everything, but *this time was different... my heart knew.*

She offered to give me the cards he'd sent her, so I went to her house and picked them up. This time, I would have proof. I did not pray about it; I didn't talk to God. I just went.

She stayed near my grandmother's house, so I packed the girls up, took them to my granny's, and went to look the woman in the face who was having an affair with my husband.

My thoughts were racing, but something in me wouldn't even let me cry or react at this point. It was stupid of me to go—it was at night,

I was alone, and anything could have happened. I pulled up, got out of the car, and met her as she was walking to the car.

Driving over, I wondered what she would look like. A part of me envisioned that she was fat and ugly. To my displeasure, she was a very beautiful young woman, much younger than I was at the time. Despite how pretty she was, another part of me still pictured *my hands around her throat, choking the life out of her.*

She handed me the small stack of stuff, and I took it. She said something sarcastically polite like, *"You're a very nice person."* I looked at her and just walked away. *It wasn't worth it.*

I drove around, wondering where to stop so I could look at this stuff without being seen. I went several blocks away and pulled over. I opened the first card, and sure enough, it was my husband's handwriting—sweet, loving words to another woman.

I cannot find the words to describe how I felt. It was like something punched me in the stomach. That night, something in me died. These were words I longed for him to say to me. It hurt me to my core—to think that while I was carrying his child, he was emotionally and physically involved with another woman.

I was angry, disappointed, and experiencing every emotion a wife in this situation could feel.

While I sorted through my feelings, I kept a brave face for people. Some knew, others speculated, and some had no idea. This was hard. I couldn't think clearly; I felt stuck. *Do I stay? Do I leave? I have two small children.*

After some time, I decided I wanted to fight for my marriage. I was angry with him for cheating, disrespecting our marriage and home, and for letting the enemy come in. But I was even angrier at the devil for trying to take what belonged to me.

Every day, I focused on forgiving and tried to do what I could to put the pieces back together. I'd like to tell you that we worked through it and came out victorious, but that didn't happen. *Stick with me—there's more to this.*

Perhaps you've already been able to connect with me on some of this, and if not, keep reading, because I'm praying that something I share will relate to you. My prayer is not only that you can relate, but that you will be touched and inspired by my story. My prayer is that my story will ignite positive change in your life, that you will learn to know God in a new or better way, and that you will come to understand—if you don't already—that God has a plan for your life regardless of what you may go through.

This is not a sad, sob pity party, but honey, *there is victory in this* for me and for you. My Pastor says, *"A disappointment is not a missed appointment."* Let's go ahead and put an amen right here.

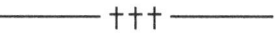

Needless to say, after this, I was really seeking God. I was seeking Him for guidance, healing, and sanity—I just needed God. My words to my husband were, *"You let the devil in, now you've got to fight like hell to get him out."* A part of me shut down completely. I never wanted to allow myself to be that vulnerable again. I never wanted to hurt like that again; the pain was overwhelming. I had decided that nobody would be allowed to hurt me like this again.

We had a counseling session with his Pastor and First Lady once, and I guess he felt that was enough. I was emotionally exhausted and really didn't know what else to do, so I focused on trying to improve myself and be a good mother to my children. I concentrated on ministry and tried to make the best of the situation.

Before long, we were back to the same routine. *Where was God in all of this? How could we be so successful in ministry but fail in our own home?*

Although my marriage was difficult, I did everything I could to stay faithful and committed to praying for him. There were moments when I was home and my husband was away that I could feel the enemy's presence very strongly. I would immediately pray and rebuke the devil.

As I drew closer to God, those moments deepened my sensitivity to His Spirit and His voice. I began to notice that prayer was often stirred by something beyond myself. Over time, I also became more aware of the spirit realm, and my dreams became a part of that awareness. I would dream dreams and then journal them, even when I didn't fully understand their meaning. Some dreams were so vivid and disturbing that they lingered with me long after I woke up. *I often asked God why He allowed me to see things I couldn't yet interpret,* but I came to realize that if a dream stayed with me, it must hold significance.

It wasn't just through dreams, though—sometimes I could feel in my spirit when something was wrong, even without explanation.

I remember one night when I sensed something evil nearby. I was home alone with the kids, and I began to pray and plead the blood of Jesus. Turns out, that very night, my husband was robbed at gunpoint, with a gun held to his head, and forced to beg for his life.

Cases like these taught me how to be more sensitive to the Spirit. I didn't fully understand what was happening, but *I knew something was wrong.* If you're a Spirit-filled believer, you need to pay attention to your *"knower."* The Spirit within you knows more than you do and will give you a nudge to remind you to pray. Never dismiss it as paranoia or craziness—*just pray!*

CHAPTER 09

The Silent Surrender

My dream was being attacked. The one thing I wanted most as a little girl was slipping through my fingers, but *I refused to let that happen.* I was on a mission to save my family, and no devil or woman was going to take it from me! I started to pray more and more.

By then, we had moved into our own church building. Businesses were thriving, and the church was growing. I would hear other First Ladies talk about how they prayed for their husbands and how God turned their situations around. So, I was one praying sister. But *the more I prayed, the worse things seemed to get. When I thought things were getting better, something would happen to quickly remind me that they weren't.*

One day, I was in my kitchen praying quietly when I heard God say, "Be still, and know that I am God." (Psalm 46:10, KJV) This was all He would say to me for months. I would respond, *"I am, Lord,"* or at least I thought I was.

I kept moving forward in my ministry because I wanted to serve God with excellence.

I wanted to teach God's people that He was real, that He was the true and living God, and that we needed to be in relationship with Him. It had become my passion to do my best to help God's people know Him in a genuine way.

Meanwhile, I was hoping that someday my husband would love and respect me again.

God began to reveal Himself to me in new ways. I would be preaching and look at people, sensing concern in their hearts. Sometimes, during praise and worship, the Spirit of the Lord would fall, and I would feel an unction to lay my hands on people. As I did, they would be slain in the Spirit. Afterwards, people would tease me and say, *"Y'all, Pastor Tina had a crusade again."*

This made me question whether I had done the right thing; maybe I was doing too much. But the thought that comforted me was that I knew it was right because I obeyed God, and people were healed and delivered.

I remember one time, I was gently rebuked by my husband for taking up too much time. *That hurt me.* I never wanted to be disrespectful to my husband as pastor, to the leadership, or, most importantly, to God. I was just doing what *I felt* God was telling me to do. So, I became more careful and only did what I was asked to do, then sat down.

From then on, if I felt the Spirit leading me to move forward, I would ask for permission. I didn't feel as free, but I wanted to be in order. Even when you're in a tough spot, *you must remember that God does not bless anything that is out of order.* We live in a time now where people don't want to be submissive to anyone in leadership and are often disrespectful.

THE SILENT SURRENDER

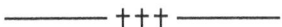

Don't get me wrong, I'm not saying you should follow someone who is corrupt and manipulative. Because, when it comes to marriage, the most popular scripture among husbands everywhere is Ephesians 5:22 (KJV): "Wives, submit yourselves unto your own husbands, as unto the Lord." It's a highlighted part of the fifth chapter, but not the whole thing. I have no problem with being submissive—any woman who loves and trusts her husband naturally does this. But the problem arises when the standard is lowered and trust is broken. *It's hard to submit to what is below you, below what you deserve.*

The same principle applies outside of marriage. Currently, America is at odds with the current administration. Many people disagree with their policies or how they handle things. But guess what? We may not agree, but we must respect their position and pray for them regardless. If you are not the Senior Pastor, you shouldn't try to usurp authority or step outside of the order God has established—no matter how wronged or hurt you may feel.

I had to learn that lesson the hard way. There were moments when my emotions wanted to take over, when I wanted to defend myself or share my side of the story. But God kept reminding me that He would vindicate me. I realized that when you operate out of order, you put more than just your peace at risk—you jeopardize your blessings. If you find yourself in that place, I urge you from my own experience: whatever you do, stay in order. Listen to and obey God. *And don't let your emotions move you out of His will.*

As a leader, people look up to and follow you. Most importantly, when Jesus's name is linked to your life, you cannot handle transitions carelessly. In these moments, it's not just about you. You're not the only one impacted, even if it feels that way. Staying in order will lead you to complete victory. It may take time, but it will happen.

———— †† † ————

Life had become *"he did his thing and I did mine,"* but we were great partners at church. I didn't nag him about it, but every now and then I'd write a letter or send him an email. Those were methods I sometimes chose because it was easier for me to express what was in my heart. It was only a momentary release, though, never a resolution. As time went on, I started to get invitations to preach at other churches. God would move in mighty ways, and I was amazed at how He used me.

I didn't start my life wanting to be a First Lady or a preacher. I simply wanted to be a wife, a mother, and have a career. But there was something about preaching that went straight into my heart and spirit. I couldn't ignore it.

Could it be my destiny? Could it be that I thought I was meant to help physical bodies recover, but God wanted me to nurture spiritual ones instead? I ran from it for a while, *but how many of you know you can run, but you can't hide? I couldn't help but throw my hands up in agreement with that truth.*

I watched my great-aunt struggle for many years as a woman minister and pastor. She faced battles that many women in ministry now benefit from. She took the heat for many of us who now have more freedom to preach the gospel in pulpits and around the world. *She accepted the call* in a Baptist church during the 1970s. This was a time when some pastors wouldn't acknowledge her or let her sit in their pulpits. They talked about her, tried to intimidate her, and even tried to take over her church. *She fought her way* into ministry to gain validation and respect.

There is still some struggle for women in ministry today, but nothing like what she endured. I admire her for her strength, fortitude, and courage in standing up for what she believed God called her to do. She obeyed God despite opposition.

She was an African American woman minister, and then God called her to pastor. She did not let others' words or actions stop her. She taught us the Word of God, holiness, and sanctification—yes, even in the Baptist church. She taught us how to love God and be fully committed to Him. I will always honor her for that. She was a role model for women preachers and one of the reasons I felt so passionate about preaching. I had to protect what others wanted to destroy. I was her legacy.

I have to be honest and say that after a while, I didn't know what else to do. I felt like I was in the marriage all alone.

Why wouldn't he fight back? Maybe he felt I wasn't worth fighting for. And that made me question if I was doing something wrong.

When I traveled, I looked forward to being among women in leadership at conferences. At these events, they held classes, and I always arrived eager to listen and learn because I desperately needed guidance. I hoped and prayed I would find answers.

Unfortunately, most of the time, I left those sessions feeling like something was wrong with me—*like there must be something about me that made God unwilling to rescue my marriage or hear my prayers. I was crushed inside.* Sitting in those sessions with women I thought I could relate to, the things they said made it seem as though I was the only one with issues. They would say their husbands had never cheated on them. They talked about how they prayed, and God turned things around for them. I hesitated to say anything because I remember everyone came in smiling and seemed so happy. *Was I the only one who was terribly unhappy?*

They talked about typical challenges: husbands not spending enough time with you or the kids, putting the church first, nosy members, or potential homewreckers. They discussed knowing your place in the ministry—like not every wife is called to co-pastor, that kind of thing. Everyone seemed to have it all figured out. They prayed, and everything went smoothly for them. Yet, I always left feeling empty and even more insecure.

I understand that as the wife of a leader, you cover him. But looking back, I feel it's like a prison—a place that isolates you from sharing and seeking wisdom from others. *Who do you trust?* When it's something you believe your spouse has done wrong, you can't even share it with your mentors or pastors, because you don't want to expose them. *Who comforts you, when the very ones who normally would, can't?*

And because of that, you end up carrying the weight of this burden alone, all while trying to move forward. People see the smile on your face, *but inside, your heart is aching and being torn apart.* You keep serving while broken, *because nobody can know.* Later, you find yourself praying to God to lift the burden, holding on to the hope that things will get better with time.

Well, I have learned that you cannot move forward or heal while carrying burdens you are not meant to carry. Even if you think you are being honorable and a dutiful wife, *you are dying on the inside.*

If I am talking to you, you need to find a confidant, a friend. If you can't find someone who is proven trustworthy, then even if you have to pay a professional who is legally bound to keep your confidence, do it. But you have to talk to somebody.

I know how you feel. I've been there. I still feel like I am somewhat there, even as I write this book, because part of me still feels I should cover them. Don't allow the enemy to back you into a corner. He wants to get you to a place where you feel completely alone, so he can beat you until you are too exhausted to fight. *Everyone needs somebody.*

The things I share about my life are not to harm or discredit anyone. It's my story. I lived it. I know what I have endured. I know the tears I've shed and the heartache I've faced. I know my mistakes. God knows. I can no longer stay completely silent. After twelve years of writing, God is allowing me to share my story. *If it's just one, so be it. Then I will have been obedient and fulfilled my assignment.*

One thing you need to be careful of is that the enemy will hold you hostage with the very information you keep inside. He will taunt you and use that righteous act against you. He will use it in any way he can to tear at you, to eat at you, until he can devour you.

He will speak lies to your mind and prey on your weaknesses and insecurities. He will use the broken places in your heart to work against you. He will bind you with what you are trying to carry.

You must remember—it's not just about stopping you, it's about stopping God's plan. I was about to find myself in that very place.

CHAPTER 10

What Do You KNOW?

I read the books and I prayed the prayers, yet nothing got better—it only grew worse. Kind of like the woman with the issue of blood. After she had been taken advantage of, lost everything, and been exiled from everybody, she had to speak to herself. She didn't even speak it out loud. *Maybe it was because she had been by herself for so long, dealing with this, that she was used to being alone with her thoughts. Or maybe she didn't want anyone to try to stop her.*

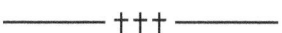

I was praying in the church one day. I had a book of prayers that another pastor's wife had just recently written. I was going to pray each prayer as she had written them, adding a little of my own words. She seemed happy, and her marriage was flourishing, *so why not give it a shot?* I was standing at the podium, maybe because it was the place where God had met me before. It was the place where I had heard His voice. *I was desperate. I needed to hear from Him.*

I stood there and began to pray. Before long, I was praying as fervently as I knew how. I went from a speaking voice, crying out to the Lord, to my voice rising and falling with the words. My hands began to clap in rhythm, my feet stomping against the floor without me even realizing it. Scripture spilled from my lips between shouts of *'Hallelujah!'* and *'Thank You, Jesus!'* The sound filled the room with the same urgency and power I remembered from my childhood. In that moment, I was praying just like my grandmother had when I was a little girl.

But then, something came over me. I went to read another line—and I could not speak. I paused in confusion. I looked back down and tried to read again, but nothing came out. Startled, I immediately began to rebuke the devil, because surely God wouldn't make me stop praying, right? I stood there, and after I calmed down, I realized the presence in the room was not evil. Still shaken, I heard the Spirit of the Lord say to me:

Do not pray another prayer for him, pray for yourself.

What?! I thought. Again, the Holy Spirit said:

Do not pray for him anymore, pray for yourself.

In tears, I closed the book and left the sanctuary.

There was a deep sorrow in me because I couldn't understand why God would not let me pray and why He wouldn't answer the prayers I had already prayed. *How could I pray and prophesy over everybody else but have no authority in my own life?*

From that day forward, I prayed for myself—asking God to show me, *me. What was it about me that needed to change or be done differently?* And every time I thought about saying anything regarding my husband, *I felt that unmistakable conviction you get when you know you are disobeying God.*

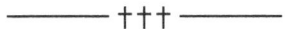

It was during this time that the word shifted for me—from "Be still, and know that I am God" to "Stand still and see the salvation of the Lord."

Why not pray? I wanted to know. When has God ever told anyone not to pray? I wanted to know the answer to that question, so I searched the Scriptures and found two places where the Lord instructed Jeremiah not to pray for the people—Jeremiah 7:16 and 11:14.

Jeremiah 7:16 (NLT) says: "Pray no more for these people, Jeremiah. Do not weep or pray for them, and don't beg me to help them, for I will not listen to you."

This was a new experience for me, but it was what God said— and it was a horrible feeling. Then, as time went on, the Holy Spirit began to reveal something to me that might be a bit controversial for some and ruffle a few feathers. He said:

You can't pray to Me against the will of another person.

He gave me a simple example. One of my favorite beverages used to be Pepsi. He said:

If someone begins to pray, 'Lord, stop Tina from drinking Pepsi, I cannot answer that prayer until you come into agreement with it.

In that moment, I realized that if you continue to pray against a person's will, you are operating in the spirit of witchcraft. You cannot pray for people to do what you want them to do or change them to be who you want them to be—even if those prayers are for what you think is their benefit. You can pray all day long for me to

NOTHING WASTED

give up Pepsi, but if it is not my desire or will to do so, God's hands are tied.

When praying for people, we have to know how to pray. Sometimes we try to pray blessings on people when God has already cursed them, or pray away consequences that God allowed for their sin.

In such cases, we must know how to pray and be clear about why we are praying what we are praying. Some prayers are offered out of selfishness—*not because we truly want the person to be better, but because we want them to be the way that will make us happy.*

Now, understand—I am not saying we shouldn't pray for people. Prayer is powerful. We can and should certainly pray for everyone. I am saying we have to be mindful of what we are praying, our motives for praying, and sensitive to what the Spirit of the Lord is leading us to pray for. We can pray for salvation, deliverance, healing, or whatever the need may be, but we must also recognize that the individual must come into agreement before those prayers can be answered.

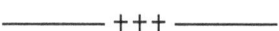

All those years God told me to "Be still, and know..." (Psalm 46:10, KJV), that He was God, He was telling me I needed to *know Him*. Many of us *know of* God, but we don't truly know Him. We know His requirements and His rules, but we don't know Him personally. Knowing Him comes through intimacy—spending time together in all seasons, not just in the good times.

Intimacy means closeness, familiarity, and friendship. This can only be obtained by living together. As much as we want to rush the process, it cannot be rushed. You have to move at the speed of your destiny. You can't have what others have, how they have it, or when they have it. What works for them may not work for you.

WHAT DO YOU KNOW?

Your process isn't someone else's process. You may be able to apply some of the same principles, but I've learned that you can pray the exact same prayer word-for-word—and if it isn't God's will for your life, it won't happen. God was teaching me who He was—His character, His ways. He was also teaching me who I was and showing me who He had created me to be. I'm still learning. I believe that no matter how long we live, it will never be enough time to know everything about Him. I believe some things about Him will only be revealed when we get to Heaven.

Of course, while He was telling me this, I was thinking, *Okay, but I need you to help me fix this.* I needed answers. I needed movement. "Be still, and know that I am God" (Psalm 46:10, KJV)—that's what I got. So, I didn't stop fighting; I just changed the way I fought. I asked Him to show me, *me.*

I loved God and wanted to make Him proud. That has always been my desire. I even reached a point where I said, *If this is how it's going to be, then at least let me live in a better house and drive a nicer car. If I have to suffer in this marriage and be unhappy, then at least let me find some happiness in something.*

It was never my desire to get divorced. But after the cars and the house, something inside me was dying every day. I felt like I was suffocating.

I struggled to believe that my life was not reflecting the goodness of God. It seemed like everything His Word declared, my life was the total opposite.

I began to think, *This can't be the will of God.* Something inside me wouldn't let me settle—no matter how much I tried.

Little did I realize that this dying feeling was me mourning my marriage and my dream more each day. *It felt like it was literally killing me.* By this time, we were physically apart. We owned properties, so he started staying at our first home—initially randomly, then more often—while I remained at the other. It was a large, beautiful new house—four bedrooms, three and a half bathrooms, a den, an office, a dining room, stunning hardwood floors, a finished basement, a patio, and a deck. It only needed a few minor updates; it was everything I had dreamed of and more. But I was there alone—just me and my kids.

This wasn't what I imagined years ago. It wasn't the vision I had. I started mourning the loss of my dreams. I cried for many days and nights. I didn't realize I was grieving at the time, *but it felt like death.*

I could feel it in my spirit—the inner bond you share when you're married had been broken at its core. It was difficult because I also had to accept that *there was nothing I could do to restore it*. But the breaking in my marriage wasn't the only dream I would have to let go of.

CHAPTER 11

The Departure

There comes a moment when leaving begins long before you ever walk out the door. In my heart, I had already begun to step away—from him, from the church, and from the life I thought I would always have. *What do you do when you think that you have everything, and in all actuality, you have nothing?* I had the cars, I had the house, but I did not have a home.

This baffled me because this was not how things were supposed to be—or was it? There were so many unanswered questions, so much frustration, and so much pain. How could the person who was supposed to be the closest to me be so far away? *Was there nothing about me that would cause a desire to fix this?*

I started to doubt my worth. I felt unworthy and inadequate. I believed I was not good enough and that I could never be the wife he needed. On the outside, I appeared beautiful and seemed to have everything under control—smiling, praising, praying, and proclaiming—*yet inside, I was falling apart. I was hurt, broken, insecure, and lonely.*

The enemy began to work overtime on me. This was his prime chance to destroy me. I had grown tired of the journey. One of my favorite messages that God gave me years ago, from Numbers 21:4 (KJV), was pulled from verse 4: *"Don't Let the Way to Your Destiny Discourage You."* How ironic. I had certainly found my way to that place. After years of infidelity and emotional abuse—trying to forgive and move on again and again—I was drained physically, mentally, and spiritually. I had no fight left in me.

This was not what God was requiring of me. I told God, *"I am not built to be his wife. If this is my ministry, I'm not anointed enough to handle this. I've surely made a mistake. It's killing me."*

I filed for divorce in 2010 when I felt lost. Maybe it was my last attempt to get his attention. Before the court date, we talked, and he seemed willing to fight for us—*or so I thought.* We agreed to discuss our issues and try counseling to fix things. Even after 18 years together, I didn't want our marriage to end and was ready to let go of the past to rebuild what we had. He said he wanted to save it too and made me believe he was just as committed. But after that talk and the court date, nothing changed. No more discussions, no actions, *just life as usual.*

Things started to fall apart for both the businesses and the church. I gave him a year, and if things didn't change, I would leave. Even though I had every legal right to end the marriage, I still asked God for permission to be released because, *even in this, I wanted to be in His will.* As I earnestly sought God, He told me:

I didn't require you to get into it. It was your desire to be married, and I honored that. He said, *It is always your choice. Whether you stay or leave, I will be with you.*

Still mourning my marriage, I decided to file for divorce again in 2011. This time, there was no turning back. No conversation.

Soon after, rumors started spreading, one that reached me in particular was about me leaving to start my own church. And the gossip—*well, you know how people can chew you up and spit you out with their words, don't you?* Then legal issues surfaced that I wasn't aware of. I had to decide to close my business because of the repercussions of the allegations against my husband.

That was deeply frustrating.

Things went from bad to worse. The court date finally arrived, and I was nervous because I had never been inside a courtroom for anything other than fulfilling my civic duty as a juror. The unknown weighed heavily on me; *I had no idea what to expect from the proceedings. I was emotional, my thoughts racing, and it felt as though my heart was in my throat.* Still, I looked forward to getting it over with.

My lawyer and I went in, but the judge refused to grant me the divorce because of a pending trial against my husband. I was in shock, then extremely angry. *I couldn't believe that after all the suffering, hurt, pain, and infidelity, I still had to go through this.* Going into that courtroom, I only had one goal—to ensure that he remained a good provider for our daughters. They deserve to be treated right and loved. Nothing else mattered. Yet, after hearing this, there was nothing I could do. I was forced to put my life on hold for another year until this was resolved.

It was during this time that I shifted from feeling exhausted, insecure, and inadequate to feeling angry. *I was angry at life. I was angry at him. I was angry with myself. And I was angry with God. Why had I sacrificed so much for someone who couldn't care less about me? Why wouldn't God work on my behalf?*

CHAPTER 12

The Darkness

Before the conversations, the paperwork, and the added disappointment, I had to face the reality of losing another dream—my career and the people I loved so dearly: the church. There had already been moments when I knew the marriage was failing, but this loss cut just as deep. I went from being an entrepreneur to *punching someone else's clock* again.

It had become my dream to expand my business to multiple locations. I wanted to make a difference in the lives of young children and their families. I spent years investing in continuing education because I wanted to perfect what God had entrusted to me.

I had been involved in childcare for nearly ten years. I started out providing care in my home during the early days of government-funded in-home childcare. At that time, it was just beginning, and while some viewed it as a way to hustle the system, for me, it was an opportunity to earn income for my family while staying home with my young daughter. I didn't want to miss any of her *"firsts."* That was my only goal at the beginning.

I didn't realize it would open my eyes to a world I had only seen in movies or heard about on the news. I met families from all walks of life. I encountered children battling anxiety, as well as those who had been abused or neglected. It broke my heart. I wanted to create a safe space for them to visit every day. Eventually, I realized that I wasn't really the "stay-at-home" type. Once my daughter started school, I wanted to get out and expand beyond my home. I prayed for a place where I could grow my business and help more kids.

When things were going well for us, we looked at a church that already had a childcare center on its premises. I was excited. Surely, this was God answering my prayer. Working in childcare was challenging—more often than not, dealing with parents was harder than managing the children—but it had become my calling, and I worked hard to make it the best it could be.

But now I had to face the reality that this was ending. At the same time, I moved out of the house I had believed God for, *a house that had everything except the white picket fence.* It was being foreclosed on and listed for sale by the bank. *The United States was deep in a recession, and it was hitting everyone hard.* Lenders threatened to repossess my car. I went from a four-bedroom, three-and-a-half-bath home to renting a two-bedroom apartment, using the den as a third bedroom so my girls could each have their own space. There was no way I could afford that place on my own.

My life was falling apart right before my eyes. All the while, I kept functioning in ministry—dysfunctional inside, but still outwardly active. I would lead praise and worship, preach, encourage others, then go home, feed my kids, ensure they were okay, and retreat to my bedroom.

I'd close the blinds and retreat to my bed, *letting sleep become my escape—an outlet made easier by sleeping pills that numbed both my thoughts and feelings.*

When the business closed, I looked for work. I hadn't been anyone's employee for almost seven years. I didn't know which way to go. A local pastor graciously hired me. The job was in a Christian environment, and it became a support for me during this hard season. Still, it was uncomfortable being in such a strange and unfamiliar place in life.

Thinking had become painful. My mind constantly raced—images, thoughts, and flashbacks played in my head nonstop. *I was no good. I was in a dark place, and no one knew.*

Everything I had worked and sacrificed for was gone. *The dream I had for my life had turned into a nightmare.* No marriage, no family structure, no home, no career. I worried about what example I was setting for those who looked up to me—especially my daughters. I wanted them to see hope, to see the love of God, to believe that living for Him meant being blessed, not broken.

Can I be honest with you? I was devastated. *The pain of just being awake was almost too much to bear.* I was constantly overwhelmed by emotional pain, and sometimes even physical pain. I knew I needed something. If nothing else could help, I hoped the Word of God would.

I didn't have the focus to read the Bible every day, but each night when I got into bed, I played the same CD—a message from Bishop T.D. Jakes' Revival Series titled *You Can Recover After a Fall.* I listened to it every night for months. I didn't realize it then, but *I believe the Word was gradually seeping into my spirit, strengthening me from within.* Many parts of that sermon spoke to me directly, and I am thankful for Bishop Jakes' ministry.

Back then, I was told not to mention anything to the church, so I stayed quiet. Even after 17 years of helping to build and establish it, I respected that request because I was not the senior pastor. The Bible says to let all things be done decently and in order. I was in a difficult place, but I needed God, so I maintained order.

We had begun holding services at another location, preparing people for the loss of our home church, which was also facing foreclosure. This was during the heart of the recession. Many churches and families were struggling. I continued attending and serving as if everything was fine because I was committed to the people.

Who abandons a ship in the middle of a storm? Leaving them was just as hard as leaving the marriage. I loved them deeply. I prayed for them even when I wouldn't pray for myself.

But I knew my time was limited, and I could no longer pay my rent. So, I moved in with my parents. I didn't want to be a financial burden to the church. The darkness deepened. I became desperate and realized I had to talk to someone—*but not just anyone. I needed someone trustworthy.*

I found a Christian therapist. *I felt like I was losing my mind.* Those sessions provided some relief because I no longer had to bear it all alone. *My mind was drained, and I needed help sorting through my thoughts.*

Then one Sunday, while in service, my head started pounding. It quickly turned into a migraine. My vision blurred, and light became painful. I went to the office to lie down and told the ministry workers to go back to service and leave me. Suddenly, I couldn't move or speak. I was present but not really there. I kept telling myself, *Tina, get up. Move your legs. Stand up.* But nothing happened.

People came in and out, speaking words I couldn't understand. My mother entered and asked if I wanted to go to the hospital. I shook my head no. After the service ended, they carried me to the car. I remember bits and pieces of the ride home, wondering if I was about to die. *Strangely, I didn't care.*

The next morning, I woke up with a dull headache but was able to move again. Soon after, my therapist recommended I see a doctor about antidepressants. I was so mentally overwhelmed that for therapy to help, I needed my mind to be stable enough to process.

I understand what some Christians might think—"Just pray and rebuke that spirit of depression." Yes, prayer works, but at that point, I wasn't in a place of faith. My struggle was with God Himself.

I felt rejected by Him. I believed I had been faithful and served well, yet it still wasn't enough. If I wasn't good enough for Him, what good was I to anyone else—especially my children? I started taking the antidepressants, my *"happy pills,"* as I called them. Over time, they helped prevent me from falling as deeply into the *darkness.*

But hopelessness is dangerous. When you feel like you have no purpose, no reason, and no hope, it's a recipe for disaster—and that's where I was. Everything I had built over 17 years was gone. In my late thirties, I should have been stable and progressing, but I was starting over. No job. No home. No husband. No church. Everything I thought defined me was gone.

I started questioning where God was. Why did He allow this? I was furious. I wanted out—out of life itself. If my life wasn't going to please Him, if He wasn't going to get the glory, *I asked Him to let me die.*

I went through the motions of life, feeling like everyone else was getting it right while I was drowning. The enemy had blinded me, and I couldn't see the light.

I started making reckless decisions, thinking, *Let's see if God will give me grace like He does for everyone else. I figured I would probably die anyway, so I might as well try to enjoy living.*

I felt hopeless, depressed, and desperate for the pain to end. People can be cruel, holding you to standards they can't meet themselves, judging without understanding. While I was in that dark place, others took advantage of what they thought was my downfall. The most painful part was that the people who knew the truth never defended me.

It left me looking like I had caused it all. That cut deeper than anything the enemy could do. My faith was unraveling. *I could believe for others, but not for myself.* The attack was on my faith because the enemy knew that destroying my faith would disarm my destiny.

"Without faith, it is impossible to please God" (Hebrews 11:6, KJV). My deepest desire has always been to please Him, but my faith was fractured. Everything I thought I knew about God was challenged in this season. *The God I had known and loved since my youth felt like a stranger.*

I didn't want to sing, pray, or preach. What could I say that would make anyone believe in the God I served when my life looked like this? I wanted relief, so I tested the waters, wondering if His grace was still for me. *I had nothing left to lose.*

And while God was all I had and I couldn't take any more, life dealt me another blow—this time it touched my family.

CHAPTER 13

The Diagnosis

Life hit again. This time it was my granny. She was diagnosed with Alzheimer's disease. Out of all the things I thought could happen, Alzheimer's was not one of them. It was not in my family line—I don't know anyone else in my family who had it. We wondered, *What is this, and where did it come from?*

My Granny, as I told you before, was a praying woman. She loved God, and somewhere, locked within the confines of her spirit, she still did. We thought it was just typical aging when she started forgetting things. *She was nearly 80 years old, after all.* At first, she began misplacing items like her purse and money, and she would lash out in anger, accusing us of stealing from her. This disease was so new to us; we didn't know what to expect. It could progress quickly or slowly.

The medication wasn't a cure—only meant to slow the progression—and its effectiveness depended on how her body responded. *No guarantees.* Some days, she seemed more like herself; other days, she was completely different. She needed to be monitored 24/7. At first, we took turns caring for her. *She was the heart of our family.*

I remember the day I went to take her out for breakfast. She hadn't been eating well, and of course, she had trouble navigating the kitchen. She was so happy when I arrived. We went to IHOP—she liked their pancakes. As I helped her into the car, I tried to engrain the moment in my mind because it could very well be the last time I could do this with her. It brought back memories of the times I used to pick her up for church. Every time she got in the car, one of the first things she did was pull the mirror down and check her face. She'd say, *"Let me see if my nose is nasty."* That always made me laugh.

That day, she kept talking and talking. I can't remember all of her words exactly, but I know she repeated some things over and over. I remember the day clearly—it was cloudy and cool, the day I helped her order pancakes and coffee. We ate, talked, and laughed.

I looked at her closely, wanting to hold onto this moment. I mentioned my marriage to her, eager to hear her wisdom. She wasn't able to give detailed advice anymore, but when I said, *"I guess I just have to trust God,"* she simply replied, *"Yeah, just trust God."*

I had the opportunity to care for her earlier when I owned my own business. I'd go over in the mornings, help her get ready, and make sure she ate something. Every day, I noticed she forgot more quickly and seemed more confused. Soon, I had to remind her who I was and even feed her because she lost the ability to feed herself.

It was heartbreaking to watch my grandmother slowly decline, and there was nothing I could do to stop it.

At first, I prayed that God would heal her. I believed He would. But as time went on, I had to accept that *He would heal her in His own way*. I treasured the moments I shared with her as she slipped away from coherence and awareness.

In her final stages, my grandmother was non-verbal, immobile, and sustained only by a feeding tube. *I still struggle to understand why God would allow her to suffer like that for so long.* It felt like her spirit was trapped in a non-functioning body. I get angry sometimes because I wanted my grandma to spend her later years in health, like others.

On June 25, 2019, the Lord called my Granny home.

I miss her voice, her laugh, her touch, her hugs, her prayers, and her wisdom. I miss her terribly.

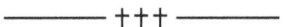

Another blow. Later, came words no one wants to hear. My mom came over to deliver the news that the doctors believed they had found cancer. They said they were 95 percent sure that the mass on her kidney was cancerous. We sat on the side of the bed and cried.

Of course, the devil started whispering thoughts into my mind: *Her mom died of leukemia. Her dad died of cancer. Now her?* In that moment, we were scared. But the only words I could get myself to say were, *"We must trust God."* I believed with everything in me that He would heal her—for her. *She had been faithful to Him and to His ministry.*

I knew I had to stay strong for her. I gathered enough strength to stand with her during this process. She would need surgery to remove the mass. Once it was taken out, they could test it to identify the type of cancer and determine the next treatment steps. Surgery was scheduled a week before Christmas.

My mom had a horrible experience with a previous surgery, and she was really scared about being cut again. I did my best to reassure her that it wouldn't be like last time and that everything would be okay. *It had to be. It's tough seeing your mom go through something like this.*

As they rolled her out of the room that morning, my dad went with her. I was left in the room praying for the Lord to *please have mercy, heal her, and not take her from me yet.*

The surgery was long, but it went well. They removed her kidney, performed a biopsy, and their 95 percent estimate turned into 0 percent—*no cancer! They had been so sure, but God.* Once again, God proved Himself to be a healer in my family.

She was left without a kidney, but she had her life. *To God be the glory!* She came home a few days later. I had only two days to go Christmas shopping for my kids. Somehow, I managed, and the girls and I spent Christmas Eve at my parents' house. *It was one of the best Christmases I've ever had.* But even in the midst of joy, life still had its challenges waiting for me.

CHAPTER 14

The Invitation

Although life was still tough, I started moving forward. During that process, I began engaging in conversations with people I shouldn't have. People I knew didn't have good intentions for me. They used my pain against me, and I let it happen. I just wanted the pain to stop.

The thing about that is, *God kept me in it. Wow.* When I think about what might have been, even in my foolishness, God kept me. Even when I was angry with Him and told Him *not to speak to me*—He still kept me. When I thought He had turned His back on me and left me, I didn't realize then that He was there all along. I will praise Him for the rest of my life for that alone.

He didn't allow me to be defiled by my own stupidity because He knew He wasn't finished with me yet.

Even though I was done and threw in the towel, *He caught it and held on for a while because He was still preparing me for my destiny—and in time, He would throw it back.*

While I was in this place, someone I knew from a distance tried to befriend me. I was harsh with him at first because he was also a preacher, and it reminded me of where I had just come from. Still, he would check on me from time to time. I'd answer quickly and leave it at that. *I wondered why he was interested in me. What did he want? Why was he here? If I ignored him long enough, maybe he would go away.*

I believe people come into our lives for a reason. Some are sent by God, and others, well, they are sent by the enemy. But even if someone is sent by the enemy, I believe God can still use them to fulfill His purpose in your life. So, I always ask myself why a person has shown up in my life. *What is their reason for being here? What purpose are they meant to serve in my life—or what purpose am I meant to serve in theirs?*

After being rude and cold to this man, I felt compelled to apologize—one of my patterns. I was in a broken and dark place, and my hurt was speaking for me.

Hurt speaks loud and clear. If you listen to someone talk long enough, you'll hear it. When hurt is there, it will make itself known.

I apologized and let him speak. I listened. Then I spoke, and he listened. I realized I was talking to someone other than my therapist, and *it felt different.* I was scared because it seemed like whenever I shared even a little about myself, it could hurt me again. And I wasn't sharing my deep stuff—not even with my parents.

During this period, my mindset started to change. I went from feeling angry and sorry for myself to feeling more angry and driven. I was determined to find happiness. I believed I had a right to it. I had done everything I was supposed to do, and I knew I deserved happiness. I had sacrificed for others, trying to be what they expected me to be. I thought to myself, *if God wasn't going to give me happiness, maybe He was waiting for me to step out in "faith" and make it happen myself.*

That was the attitude I took—and that's exactly what I intended to do. Around that time, the gospel singing duo Mary Mary released a song called *Go Get It,* and *I took it literally.* If I felt something could be for me, I went after it.

After all, I was almost 40. At a time when I should have been stable and prospering, *I found myself back at the drawing board. I needed to do something.*

I started convincing myself that maybe this man was the one God had sent for me. He was persistent and seemed to know the right things to say. I was on a mission to be happy. After all the hell I had gone through, surely this was my time. After such a terrible season, I longed for a season of joy. *Was this my chance for a knight in shining armor to save me from misery?* I began creating images in my mind of what life could be like with him. He had been through a similar experience, which became our common ground. Now I realize that what we shared was called a trauma bond. Our pain and past connected us.

I started thinking, *Nobody else might want you, so maybe you should give this a shot.* He was older, which I saw as a good thing because he was stable—and maybe I wouldn't have to worry about him cheating. *Crazy, right?* But that was my mindset. My self-esteem was nearly nonexistent, and for some reason, I believed this was reasonable and rational thinking.

He sent me flowers to my job every week. Sound familiar? Another pattern. Let me tell you, any man who sends me flowers to my job now—just know I'm running as far as I can. *I'm joking. Kind of.*

Looking back now, I can clearly identify the unhealthy patterns in my life. We all have them. Patterns are ways we've become accustomed to handling life. They're coping mechanisms. For me, many of my patterns were unhealthy and only took me back to the same place over and over again. *I'm still working through some of them.*

I never thought I'd be able to open my heart to anyone again, but if I wanted to be happy, I had to take a chance. I took my happiness into my own hands. *I wanted God to bless my decision—even if it wasn't His will. Maybe He would permit it as His permissive will.* Besides, I wasn't doing anything wrong; I wanted a family.

This was my second chance—not a traditional family, but I was willing to accept what I could get.

I pictured myself living the dream in the South, where I wanted to move. I wanted a fresh start. From the beginning of the relationship, he made it clear that marriage was the goal. We became friends. I finally had someone to confide in, someone who seemed to care about me. We had fun together. He made me smile again.

Although my divorce had just been finalized, I reminded myself that I had been physically separated for three years and emotionally and intimately separated for over a decade.

With that in mind, I didn't feel like I was rushing into anything. *I thought, I'm old enough to know what I want—and why waste time?* So, I invited him in—*to the possibility I had been chasing for years, and to the hope that maybe, just maybe, this time would be different.*

CHAPTER 15

Miss Fix It

I was back in my "Prince Charming" phase, wondering if this could finally be him—if my dreams could get a second wind and maybe God was giving me what I desired. I think a part of me was afraid I would end up old and alone. *I didn't want to admit it, but in my mind, that could very well have been the case.* Who would want a woman with two kids and no career?

My dreams had been shattered, and I was trying to recreate them. I didn't care what anyone thought; my mind was made up. Herein lies the problem: when you choose your plan instead of God's plan, He is not obligated to bless it. *Regardless of how right or harmless it may seem, that doesn't mean God approves.* And, of course, *not everything good is God.*

Many of us have a habit of asking God to bless our plans without ever consulting Him about them—or even caring what His plan is for our lives. When the hand of the Lord is upon you, your life is for His glory.

I was rebelling because I thought where I was could not possibly be where God wanted me. Things felt so opposite from His Word and what I believed my life should look like.

I felt like a failure and was determined to make things right. I refused to go down like so many other women I had seen. How judgmental of me, not even knowing their stories. I was so full of pride to think God would conform to what I wanted. Who did I think I was?

I asked God to bless this union and assumed He would because marriage is a choice we make. We both loved God and His ministry. He wanted a wife. I wanted a husband. What else was there to think about? He had experience with a blended family, and that gave me some peace.

Still, I never thought I would be divorced, and I definitely never imagined I would marry a second time. That was what "other people" did—it wasn't going to be my story.

Ha! My perfect fairy tale was crumpled, ripped into pieces, and set on fire.

My happiness had been delayed—partly for reasons I allowed—but I felt I needed some joy in my life. *I believed I would be a better person and a better mom if I took care of myself.* It had always been just my girls and me. Once the boys were grown, they moved away, and the three of us became the three musketeers.

I talked to the girls about the divorce, and it wasn't a difficult transition for them because they were used to us living alone. The hardest part was no longer being part of the church and their dad's family gatherings. That change in dynamic was an adjustment. They handled it well, but when we talked about me remarrying, they were hesitant. Moving away would be even harder.

My younger daughter was fully on board—this was a big adventure for her. My oldest was conflicted. She wanted to be with me, but didn't want to leave the comfort of what she'd always known. As moving day approached, she became more reluctant, and I could tell she wouldn't be happy if I forced her to go. She was 16 and wanted to finish high school with her friends.

I wanted her with me. The best place for her, in my mind, was with me. But for her happiness, I had to let go of what I wanted. I gave her the choice, thinking she would reluctantly say, "Okay, Mommy, I'll come with you." Instead, without hesitation, she said, *"I'm staying here."*

My heart sank.

How could I be completely happy without my baby? I thought she might change her mind once we got settled, but she didn't. After the conversations and giving my daughter the option to finish high school with her friends, she was only willing to come with me to be part of the wedding and for occasional visits.

I was ready for my happily ever after; however, the closer the day came, the more I started questioning the whole thing.

The day before my wedding, I still wasn't completely sure if this was really what I wanted. Then I got a call from a friend who had gone through a divorce with similar struggles. They shared their testimony and the wonderful experience of marriage the second time around. At that moment, it felt like a breath of fresh air. It reassured me, and I felt good about my decision again. I thought, *This will work out. This will be my forever.*

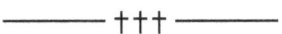

After the wedding, we took the kids to spend the rest of the summer with my parents, then tried to settle into our new normal. When summer ended, I drove down the highway to pick up my youngest daughter for school. I felt a mix of sadness and excitement—I believed I was finally stepping into happiness. I told myself I was leaving the pain of my past behind, *but the truth was, I was running from it.*

Exactly one month and one day after the wedding, we found out we were pregnant. This wasn't an accident. I wanted another baby—a boy—*because I wanted my womb to be blessed.* I know that's an Old Testament belief, but it mattered to me. I thought I might be too old to conceive or that it would take time, so I was surprised it happened so quickly.

However, it didn't take long to remember how sick I had been with my previous pregnancies, and I hoped it wouldn't be as bad this time. I was in a new place, far from family and friends, and expecting for the first time in 11 years. *Emotionally and mentally, I still wasn't healthy.*

I think my husband hadn't counted the cost of marrying me. Maybe he thought he could fix me. He couldn't. Being with him gave me hope and pulled me out of my darkest place, *but it didn't heal me.*

As soon as I found out I was pregnant, I stopped taking all my medications. I didn't want to risk my baby's health. Being pregnant made me rely on God once again. I tried to find my faith, praying I wouldn't get as sick as before. Spiritually, I was in a strange place. I loved God and never stopped loving Him—even when I felt rejected by Him—but I didn't trust Him.

We would go to church, and when the Spirit fell, I felt Him, but it seemed distant. This troubled me deeply. Losing material things was one thing, but losing God felt unbearable. I cried out for mercy, asking Him to forgive my selfishness. If I was going to survive this season, I needed Him.

Soon, sickness set in, and I was barely functioning. I went into survival mode. My husband took over everything—shopping, cooking, and dropping off my daughter at school. Uselessness crept in. Most days, I could barely get out of bed. When he left for the day, I'd lie there in tears, silently crying, *Lord, help me.*

In my weakness, I still prayed selfishly: *Lord, please let this be a boy.* I didn't deserve to ask for anything, but I wanted to know if He still heard me—*if His hand was still on my life.*

At the ultrasound, the doctor didn't have to say it—*I could tell.* It was a boy. Joy flooded me. God had honored my request. After everything, He still loved me. He still cared. *And in that moment, I realized my healing had begun.*

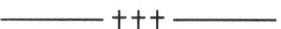

Tensions rose at home. My kids struggled adjusting to this transition. Being separated from one another for the first time. One being in a whole new state and the other back home without us. We tried to settle in and adjust to our new normal, but it proved to be a complicated process. I often felt torn between them and my husband. *It was a painful place to be, and I didn't have the strength to be strong for anyone—not even myself.*

After my son was born, I longed for a support system. My husband traveled often, and I wanted to be there for my oldest as she prepared to graduate. We discussed my going back home for a while. He didn't like the idea because he didn't want a long-distance relationship. This would be temporary, so I didn't see it as problematic. He didn't agree but said he would support my decision. *I thought we'd survive the separation.*

Three months later, he decided he wanted out. I was blindsided. *Divorced again. Rejected again.* Back in this place, 17 months after ending a 17-year marriage.

I started looking inward—at the girl I was before all my relationships. She had insecurities, was naive, and lived in a fantasy

Her faith was real, but her understanding of life was not.

Healing required me to stop blaming others and take responsibility for my choices. I asked God to show me myself—my motives, my patterns. He revealed that some things I thought were for Him were really for me, *for my validation.*

I learned that my identity was not defined by my title or position. My purpose was not *in* people but *for* people. *God showed me the truth about myself, and I had to acknowledge it.*

Even with all our flaws, *nothing can separate us from His love.* He will take our mistakes and turn them into messages and miracles. *That is why I am sharing my story. And in every part of it, God was revealing Himself to me.*

CHAPTER 16

Religion to Relationship

As I reflect back, I see that all along the way, God was teaching me who He was. At the most critical time, when I thought He had left me—when I thought He had rejected me—was actually when He was revealing Himself to me in ways I had not known. He had to let my religious perception of Him die in order to resurrect the truth of who He was in me. Every step was divinely orchestrated to perfect the things concerning me.

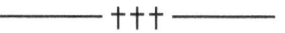

The enemy will use whatever he can to stop the plan of God for your life. He doesn't cause everything—most things we go through are because of our own decisions—but the enemy will come in and manipulate the dysfunction and the sin.

Many times, while we are drowning in hurt and pain, he's speaking in our ears, telling us everything but the truth. Remember, he is the father of lies and can't tell the truth if he wanted to. The enemy will work that hurt, that disappointment, that betrayal, that

NOTHING WASTED

pain—all to his advantage—to get you to a place where you begin to question God and doubt His plan for your life.

That is why it is so important that we are rooted and grounded in the Word of God. The Word is our defense. David said, "Thy word have I hidden in my heart, that I might not sin against thee" (Psalm 119:11, KJV).

I found that with every lie the enemy told me, the Word of God would come up against it.

I would think, "This is too much; I can't handle this," and the Word would say, "I can do all things through Christ who gives you strength" (Philippians 4:13, KJV).

I would think, "I should just end it all," and the Word would say, "The Lord gave, and the Lord hath taken away" (Job 1:21, KJV).

I'd think, "It's over," and the Word would say, "All things work together for good to them that love God" (Romans 8:28, KJV).

The Word kept speaking.

I felt like God had rejected me, and the enemy played on that, doing everything to make me doubt. I didn't realize until I was in this place that the fight was not about my happiness or keeping me from having the things I thought I wanted—it was against my faith. The enemy knew that if I lost my faith, I would lose the fight. He was working overtime on me. I was in a place where I couldn't understand what had gone wrong. How could I have prayed, fasted, preached, praised, served, and still end up in a place completely contrary to what I had worked so hard for?

When I tell you, my carnal and spiritual mind struggled to comprehend this. I believed God and His Word, and here I was left with nothing. This didn't resemble God. This didn't look like the promise. It looked like everybody else got it right—how could I have gotten it so wrong?

I know I've been repetitive with these statements, but this was a repetitive thought. It wasn't God, so it must have been me.

The devil beat me up with this:

You are not all you thought you were.

You are not anointed.

You have no power.

Look at you—what can you say to anybody now?

You don't have anything to show.

Is this what the goodness of the God you serve looks like? I started to entertain the lies, and before I knew it, I was in such a deep depression that I didn't care about living.

Then came the stupid decisions. A place of *"I don't care"* is a bad place to be in. People say all the time, *"Don't give up"* and *"Hold on."* I've said it. I've preached it. But I can honestly tell you that I had given up.

If the first divorce wasn't bad enough, here I was, divorced again and a single mother of three! I mean, really, God?

I was worse off than before I tried to fix it. I was depleted and exhausted physically, mentally, and spiritually. I would occasionally attend church, but I mostly stayed home and slept. This was the way I coped.

Who could I reach out to? Who would understand? The embarrassment and the shame consumed me. I retreated into myself.

I spent months beating myself up and basking in the lies of the enemy. Here I was again, alone with less than I had when I left the first time. I pretty much disappeared on purpose. I went silent.

I was thankful for my kids, but I felt like a total failure. I felt I had disappointed my kids, my parents, and everyone who ever looked up to me.

Here came the enemy again. He worked on me so hard—all day, every day. Images of my failures continually played in my mind over and over like a movie. He beat me up as much as I let him, because I didn't feel worthy or like much of anything.

Growing up, I felt like I was just as good as anyone else. I felt like I deserved the best. Now here I was, all these years later, having done what I thought was the right thing most of my life, and I was left with nothing to show for it.

The enemy even used the time I was diagnosed with an infection—and could no longer breastfeed my son—as ammunition to convince me I would never be good enough. Maybe you can relate to how, in your challenging situations, you struggled with the lies of the enemy.

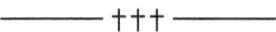

One of the most disheartening things about most people—even in the body of Christ—is that when our brothers and sisters find themselves in difficult places, for whatever reason, people are quick to believe the worst and leave you to suffer alone.

Not only will they leave you, but they will also spread rumors about you. Even if there is truth to the story, a true believer is supposed to lift up one another—because today it is me, but tomorrow it might be you.

Many of the people I supported in ministry, to this day, I have not heard from. I felt that there were people who took sides, and in doing so, contributed to the suspicion surrounding the rumors. It is interesting to me how relationships change when you no longer have anything people can benefit from.

People will make you think you are the best thing since sliced bread, but they'll leave you in a heartbeat. I can count on one hand the people who still trusted the God in me when I was unsure of myself. The enemy tried to cause bitterness to set in my heart. I was both hurt and offended. Forgiveness was the most challenging lesson I learned through this experience.

One day, while sitting on the side of the bed, I felt really down and could sense the enemy's strong suppression. I would just sigh over and over again for no reason—that was how much pressure I felt on the inside.

How was I going to take care of my kids and provide for them? How could I help my parents? I should be taking care of them now. I did not know how I was going to get through and come out of this.

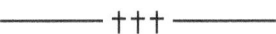

One Sunday, my mom came in from church and saw my face. It was in that moment that she saw past the natural, and she saw me. She came in and began to pray. My dad took the baby and prayed.

She prayed and prayed, then began to call me by name. Every time she called my name, something shook in me. She pleaded with me, saying, "Come on, Tina, come out of it." Something began to break in me. I could feel the struggle in my spirit. I was trying, but there was a spirit of oppression on me.

After several minutes of praying, she shouted my name again—"Tina!"—and something broke. I began to cry out. It was such a sound that I had never heard come out of me. That Sunday, in my room, God delivered me. For a second time, God used my mother to birth me into a new place in life.

The deliverance was instant, but of course, I had to go through the processes of forgiveness and being restored. I am so thankful to God for praying parents.

For some reason, God was not done with me. If you can relate to the heaviness of the oppression of the enemy—maybe it's where you are right now—I want you to know that deliverance is available for you! You don't have to stay in bondage when Christ came so that we can be free.

I want you to pray this prayer:

Lord, please help me. Your Word says that You are a very present help in the time of need. I need Your help. I need You to deliver me.

Release me from the oppression; release the hold that the enemy has on my life. Satan, the Lord rebuke you in Jesus' name. Your time is up—take your hands off of me right now.

I believe and receive my freedom in the mighty name of Jesus, I pray. Amen.

Whom the Son of Man sets free is free indeed. Glory to God!

Sometimes you need help, and that's okay. Get to someone who can help you, get with other believers, or go to your local church so you can remain free and be strengthened.

I was able to function now. I was able to catch my breath. But the shame of my past was at the forefront, and I didn't even know it. Shame was controlling my behavior. I thought I was just being humble, but it was the shame that caused me to shrink and dumb myself down in the presence of others. I needed to let go and come out of the shame of my past. I was so ashamed of myself.

Ashamed of the failures, ashamed to be a divorcee, ashamed of the financial struggles, ashamed to be a single mom. I was ashamed that I had let young girls down who looked up to me.

I was determined to show people that I was going to make a comeback, and I got knocked right back down. How stupid was I? How could I face anyone ever again? *So much shame and embarrassment.*

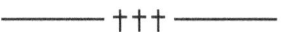

One day, I read a book by Christine Caine entitled *Unashamed*. This book helped me identify that what I was feeling was shame, and it propelled me toward being delivered. I had to stop beating myself up over the decisions I made. I needed to forgive to heal and let go of the shame.

One day, I was regretting what I had been through. I thought, *if I had done this differently, I could have had a different outcome.*

Then the Spirit reminded me:

Don't you regret another day what you have been through. In everything, I have been with you. For it was there that I watered the seed I planted. It was there that I cultivated and nourished My plan.

It was there that you discovered Me, and you got glimpses of what I wanted and planned for you to do. It was there that I introduced you to the gifts of My Spirit, and you saw miracles, signs, and wonders.

It was there that I birthed you into a deeper realm of prayer and intercession. It was there that you learned of Me and got to know Me.

Don't regret any of it, even your mistakes. Your steps are ordered. Keep walking.

So, I had to forgive and release all offenses. The hardest part of this was forgiving myself. I had to acknowledge that I was not the perfect girl I strived to be, and my story was not going to be the one I had once dreamed of. I had to let it go—let go of my dream—and learn to accept my reality. But letting go wasn't instant; it would become a process of forgiveness I had to live out day by day.

CHAPTER 17

The Reset

Forgiveness was a process for me. After years of rehearsing all the offenses, I was finally tired of it. I was ready to let it go. It wasn't who I was; it was what I had been through. I found the toughest part of forgiving was forgiving myself—for the decisions I had made, the things I allowed, for being naïve, for not being smarter, for accepting being treated in ways that were abusive, for staying too long, for settling, for not having the perfect life, for not living my dream. I had to forgive myself.

I was disappointed in myself. I wanted to make my parents proud and be proud of myself for something.

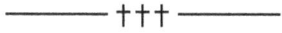

My life has a purpose, and I couldn't let unforgiveness hinder me from it. Your life has purpose as well, so you can't get stuck in unforgiveness.

Whether you are holding on to what somebody else did or didn't do, or if you won't let yourself off the hook, I want to tell you that it is time to let it go. Stop allowing the enemy to drag you down the same road over and over again. If God can throw it into the sea, never to be brought up again, and He is the only one that really matters, you can forgive. *It's not a feeling—it's a decision.*

Everything starts with a thought. *As a man thinketh in his heart, so is he.* Once you begin to think about forgiveness, forgiveness will show up. Soon after, your emotions will follow. You will then discover that when something prompts a memory from your past, it won't have power over you anymore.

In today's popular language, we might say that once you walk in forgiveness, memories won't "trigger" you anymore.

I know what it is like to be hurt to the core—the kind of hurt that goes from your throat to the pit of your belly. I know the kind of hurt that knocks the wind out of you, that causes the type of cry where you struggle to take a breath and feel like you're dying because it hurts so deeply. It is possible that even what caused that kind of pain can be forgiven.

Can I tell you that you will never have all the answers? Sometimes the *whys* have absolutely nothing to do with you. The *whys* will wear you out. You have to accept that it happened, and it happened to you. Process it, and forgive.

I've heard many people say forgiveness is not for the offender, but for you—and I agree. Most times, while you are holding on to the offense and the pain of it, the offenders are going on with their lives, living out their dreams, happy as can be.

If you find yourself stuck, pray and ask God to help you forgive. He will begin to show you the ways His love and grace were, and still are, sufficient for you.

The Lord placed me in a ministry when my faith was at an all-time low—a place I wouldn't have chosen for myself. A place called

Faith Builders International Ministries. I knew I needed a spiritual covering.

I was not sure at first why God told me this was where He wanted me. I surely thought I should be with my family or friends. Several of my family members and some friends are pastors of churches.

I could have started a church like some other co-pastors in ministry who have found themselves divorced. Although, for me, I would have needed God to come directly down from heaven to tell me that one. I certainly do not take the responsibility of pastoring the Lord's church lightly.

But God is strategic. He does not work like we think He should. I did not know how to *be*. It was difficult for me to find my place after being in leadership for so long.

It was uncomfortable for me. I was not seeking a position or to be involved in anything. Actually, it was uncomfortable and comfortable at the same time. I didn't want any responsibility.

I was satisfied with just having the option to come to Sunday service and leave. I wanted to just sit, be in the presence of the Lord, and listen to the Word. That's what I did. God emphasized the need for my faith to be rebuilt—and this time on a more solid foundation. This time, it was being built on experience and relationship. I thank God for the opportunity to serve and be a part of this ministry.

I am grateful for the Word of God that my pastors have spoken over the years. Those words have been life to me and have been the mortar to the restructuring of my faith.

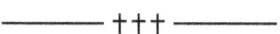

In May of 2015, my pastor prophesied a word of restoration over me. He didn't know my story, but God used him to prophesy, and that word let me know it was not over. I have humbly accepted the position of servant. That is who I am. Who I always was. And who God created me to be.

As I approach the end of this book, I have found it challenging to find an exciting conclusion. One reason is that most of the time, when you read a book by someone who has been through similar experiences, they have an ending that sounds incredible.

Like, *I was poor and now I'm rich,* or *I went through hell but I've found my "Prince Charming"—100 steps to living the dream—you know,* happy endings. We love happy endings. A happily-ever-after.

Well, I don't have that kind of ending to give you. I would love to tell you that after all this, God sent me my knight in shining armor—or that I built my dream home from the ground up and installed a white picket fence. That my children are perfect angels, that I'm living my dream, and... that I won the lottery. Wait, the saints don't do that. Scratch that part out.

That is not my ending. And honestly, that's encouraging to me, because it means God is not finished yet.

What God has done is reconcile me back to right standing with Him. He forgave me. Picked me up. And put me back on my feet. He has revealed Himself to me in ways I did not know. He has revealed things to me—about myself, and about the Scriptures. I am in awe of Him. Once I was back in a proper relationship with Him, He set me on a different path.

I went back to school and earned a degree in real estate. God, once again, strategically orchestrated my steps. Not only did I buy a home on my own, but I was the realtor on the sale.

Even in the home-buying process, after several offers were declined, I began to feel discouraged. I knew I had heard God, and then a house came back on the market with a reduced price. I asked

THE RESET

God if I should try again, and as I looked at the address, He highlighted the numbers to me. They represented the year I lost it all and the year I was restored.

Recently, my middle daughter was playing one of her final college basketball games. As I was sitting there reflecting on her 12-year basketball career, the Lord spoke to me and said, *"Nothing was wasted."* The Lord even kept my kids in mind in all of this. She discovered her love for basketball during one of the toughest times she faced as a child. God used everything. All of it.

I am just a girl who loved God and dreamed of living the typical American dream, whose life is far from perfect. I get up every morning, go to work, come home, try to be the best mom I can be, and serve my local church.

I am working hard to hear—and more so to obey—the voice of the Lord. I know that if I keep putting one foot in front of the other, if I keep praying and reading my Word and declaring what the Word says in faith, then in time the miracles will manifest.

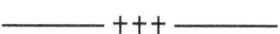

God said this to me:

Trying to be happy should not be your priority. For you, being holy should be your priority. If you make holiness your priority, then I, God, will make your happiness My priority. I didn't just put you here to be happy; I put you here to be holy.

Make me walk along the path of your commands, for that is where my happiness is found. (Psalm 119:35, NLT)

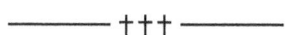

There are days that are still challenging for me. I still have to fight the spirit of depression—when things are not looking up, or I have too many consecutive bad days, when money is low, or I'm having moments of loneliness. Those feelings of depression and despair try to sneak back in, but this time I know the weapons may be formed, but they will not prosper. They don't shake my faith.

In these times, I must be more diligent in reminding myself of what God has promised and what the Word of God says for my life. We have become so accustomed to getting things quickly that we want everything to be fast, but I've learned that we must be able to endure the process of life.

The scripture teaches us that weeping may endure for a night, but joy will come in the morning. I know it's easier said than done, but you have to fight to hold on until morning. Morning will come. It has to—because God said it.

I have come to accept and embrace my story, my journey. I never quite fit the mold anyway.

I'm not easily impressed with people or things. Don't allow someone else's definition of success to govern your life. Many people are giving up and feeling inadequate because it doesn't seem to meet the criteria of what's on social media, or they feel less than because their life doesn't look like what many others are posting. Be the authentic you.

I have forgiven myself and love the woman that I have become. I embrace my flaws and everything I went through. With an open mind, eyes to see, and ears to hear, I await the challenges that come—because they will come.

I understand that I am more than a conqueror through Christ Jesus, and there is absolutely nothing too hard for Him to handle. I love and I cherish the presence of God in my life—how He loves me and speaks to me. I may not have the dream or be living the life I thought I should have, but I am grateful to be alive! I thank God for my children and my family. I am grateful for the lessons learned.

I have learned that in this life, the enemy doesn't fight fair. He indeed comes to steal, kill, and destroy, and he will use whatever he can to succeed in stopping you—even your dream. But Jesus said He came that we might have life, and life more abundantly (John 10:10, KJV). When life happens to you, don't blame God—after all, He is the one you will need to make it through.

Just because your plans may not have worked out doesn't mean your purpose is over. Many are the plans in a man's heart, but it is the Lord's purpose that prevails.

We can get so discouraged because of the things that go wrong and miss the things that are right—especially if you are one who has said, *"Lord, let Your will be done in my life."* You have set yourself up for an unpredictable, but awesome journey.

I don't want anything that is not in God's will for me. I don't want to be any place that He is not. Only what we do for Christ will last. I don't seek to be famous; I seek to be found faithful. I don't long for a platform; I want to be pleasing in His sight. I am confident of this, that He who has begun the work will complete it.

I don't know where you are in your life—whether you are living what you feel is your dream or you have had to re-dream several times. God knows right where you are. He created us all on purpose, with a specific purpose in mind. When your plans fail, let His plan come forth.

I have divorced my dream, and my dream has now become His dream.

"For I know the plans I have for you," says the Lord. "They are plans for good and not for disaster, to give you a future and a hope." (Jeremiah 29:11, NLT)

Amen.

CONCLUSION

Can I Pray for You?

Father, in the name of Jesus, I ask that the person reading these words has, in some way, been enlightened and encouraged by Your goodness through my story. I pray that You meet them at the very place of their need—whatever that may be.

Perhaps if they picked up this book out of curiosity—let Your glory be revealed, and let them see You.

Maybe they were searching for someone to relate to—Lord, I pray that as they turned these pages, they discovered they are not alone, that all is not lost, and that there is still hope and a life worth living.

If their life has taken a different course and things haven't worked out as planned, remind them they can trust and depend on You. Lord, heal every broken place, restore what was lost, and make them whole.

In Jesus' name I pray.

Amen.

ACKNOWLEDGMENTS

In Everything Give Thanks

God, I am so grateful for it all. Thank You for each season of my life—for every time You've carried me, counseled me, and corrected me. Thank You. My life is in Your hands.

Mom and Dad, thank you for every sacrifice you made for me. Thank you for loving me, believing in me, and being proud of me through it all. I am so blessed God gave me both of you.

To my children, I'm so grateful to God for each one of you. It is my life's pleasure to be your Mommy. Thank you for your love and support.

Thank you to my pastors for consistently preaching and teaching the Word of God. It was through your obedience to God and leadership that the Lord was able to rebuild my faith on a sure foundation.

Finally, thank you to my editor and publisher. You brought what I had written over the course of 12 years to light. Thank you for handling my story with dignity and respect. Your gifts and talents are appreciated.

ABOUT THE AUTHOR

Catina Vaughn

Catina Vaughn is a devoted mother of three and a woman whose life reflects resilience, faith, and perseverance. With years of experience in commercial property management and realty, she understands both the challenges and the opportunities that come with building and rebuilding a life. Her greatest joy, however, comes from her deep love for God and her commitment to inspiring others through her testimony.

When she is not working or writing, Catina treasures time with her children, her family, and her church community. Her prayer is that her journey encourages others to trust God with their own story and to believe that even in seasons of loss, nothing is ever wasted.

www.ingramcontent.com/pod-product-compliance
Lightning Source LLC
Chambersburg PA
CBHW020940090426
42736CB00010B/1206